Shakespeare:

An Active Approach

BRENDA PINDER

CollinsEducational

An imprint of HarperCollinsPublishers

Published by
CollinsEducational
77–85 Fulham Palace Road
Hammersmith
London W6 8JB

First published in 1990 by Unwin Hyman Ltd.
Published (reprinted) by CollinsEducational in 1992
Reprinted 1993

British Library Cataloguing in Publication Data
Pinder, Brenda
    Shakespeare : an active approach.
    1. Drama in English. Shakespeare, William, 1564–1616
    I. Title
    822.33

ISBN 0 00 322305 1

Designed by Joyce Chester
Illustrations © Peter Kent
Typeset by Acūté, Stroud, Glos.
Printed in Great Britain by Alden Press Ltd., Oxford
Bound by Hunter & Foulis Ltd., Edinburgh

Contents

Nearly all the activities can be used with any play. The plays listed here are, first, the ones featured on the students' pages followed by those mentioned additionally in the teacher's notes (bracketed).

Introduction

This book springs out of a conviction that many teachers, like myself, are dissatisfied with traditional methods of A-Level teaching, particularly of Shakespeare texts. We all try to take students to the theatre to see productions, and of course this helps, but it is all too easy to plough through the text lesson after lesson, pausing only for occasional discussions. What they can often miss is the theatricality of the script – that it is a play first and a text afterwards – and the activities in this book are intended to open this up, while at the same time directing students back to the script itself to search for evidence and reference.

Almost all the exercises here are equally applicable to any Shakespeare text, though they are usually tied to one specific example. It is simple to adapt them to any play being studied and the Teacher's Notes often suggest how this can be done.

The activities are arranged in groups, those on any one play together, except for the General Section, which contains exercises not tied to any one specific text (and often materials on more than one).

My thanks to all those teachers who have given me ideas and especially to the 'Shakespeare in Schools' Project.

Brenda Pinder

1 • *Freeze Frames*

FOCUS ON: RELATIONSHIPS/REVISION

WHOLE CLASS/GROUP WORK

KNOWLEDGE OF PLAY REQUIRED

Procedure

There are two good warm-ups for this exercise:

Statues and sculptors: In pairs, students take it in turns to mould each other into symbolic figures of abstract qualities like Greed, Pity, Anger and Power, and then into symbolic statues of the main characters in the play.

Holiday postcards: Students, in threes or fours, present in a tableau a holiday scene symbolic of the place, for others to guess.

These opening activities are designed to get students to think of the freeze frames not as 'stills' from an imaginary production but as symbolic tableaux, each of which encapsulates something about character and relationships at that moment in the play.

To prepare the freeze frames, photocopy and cut up the relevant sheet, to make cards, each with a line from a particular moment. Groups, containing the number of people indicated on the card, then have to devise quickly a symbolic freeze frame to present to the whole class.

The ensuing discussion, of the placing of the characters, the gestures chosen etc., is quite as valuable as the drama activity itself and can be very useful as a revision exercise.

Examples

See accompanying sheets, one on each play.

Follow-up

Whole scenes or Acts can be presented in a series of freeze frames, e.g. 'With a limit of three freeze frames, convey the developments of the Closet scene in HAMLET.'

1 • Antony and Cleopatra: Freeze Frames

He fishes, drinks and wastes
The lamps of night in revel.

I,iv,4.

Caes.,Lep.

Thou shalt be whipp'd with wire and stew'd in
   brine,
Smarting in lingering pickle.

II.v.65

Cleo.,Charm.,Messenger.

To knit your hearts
With an unslipping knot, take Antony
Octavia to his wife.

II.ii.126.

Agr.,Ant.,Caes.,Enob.,Lep.

Vanish or I shall give thee thy deserving,
And blemish Caesar's triumph.

IV.xii.32.

Ant., Cleo.

The crown o' the earth doth melt,

IV.xv.63.

Cleo.,Ant.,Char.,Iras,

Dost thou not see my baby at my breast,
That sucks the nurse asleep?

V.ii.308.

Cleo.,Char.,Iras.

Forgive my fearful sails! I little thought
You would have followed,

III.xi.55.

Cleo.,Ant.

Being done unknown,
I should have found it afterwards well done,
But must condemn it now.

II.vii.77.

Pomp.,Menas,others.

1 • King Lear: Freeze Frames

I hear my father coming; pardon me:
In cunning I must draw my sword upon you.

II.i,28.

Edm., Edg

Hold your hand, my Lord.

III. vii.70.

Servant. Reg., Corn., Glouc.

be Kent unmannerly
When Lear is mad.

I.i.144

Kent, Lear, Cord.

henceforth I'll bear
Affliction till it do cry out itself
'Enough, enough' and die.

IV.vi.75.

Glouc., Edg.

Prescribe us not our duty.

I.i.274.

Reg., Gon., Cord.

Pray do not mock me;
I am a very foolish, fond old man.

IV.vii.59.

Lear, Cord., Kent.

If thou follow him, thou must needs wear my
coxcomb.

I.iv.101.

Fool, Kent, Lear.

Lend me a looking glass;
If that her breath will mist or stain the stone,
Why, then she lives.

V.iii.260.

Lear, Cord., Alb., Edg., Kent.

Shakespeare: an active approach   **7**

1 • Macbeth: Freeze Frames

Fail not our feast.

III.i.28

Macb., Lady Macb., Banq.

Which of you hath done this?

III.iv.47.

Macb., Lady Macb., B's Ghost, other lords.

O yet I do repent me of my fury
That I did kill them.

II.iii.104

Macb., Lady Macb., others.

Say if thou'st rather hear it from our mouths
Or from our masters?

IV.i.62.

Macb., Three Witches.

I have begun to plant thee and will labour
To make thee full of growing.

I.iv.28.

Dunc., Macb., Banq.

He that's coming must be provided for.

I.v.66.

Macb., Lady Macb.

Thou liest, thou shag-eared villain!

IV.ii.32.

Lady Macduff., Son, Murderers.

What man, ne'er pull your hat upon your brows:
Give sorrow words.

IV.iii.208.

Malc., Macd., Ross.

1 • The Tempest: Freeze Frames

And when I rear my hand, do you the like,
To fall it on Gonzalo.

II.i.290.

Ant., Seb., Alonso, Gonz.

You are three men of sin whom Destiny
. . . the never-surfeited sea
Hath caus'd to belch up you,

III.iii.53.

Ariel, Alonso, Seb., Ant., Gonz.

Mine would, sir, were I human.

V.i.20.

Ariel, Pros.

Do that good mischief which may make this
island
Thine own for ever.

IV.i.217.

Cal., Trinc., Steph.

This island's mine, by Sycorax, my mother,
Which thou tak'st from me.

I.ii.333.

Cal., Pros.

My Ariel, chick,
That is thy charge, then to the elements
Be free, and fare thou well!

V.i.316.

Pros., Ariel.

Sweet lord, you play me false.

V.i.172.

Mir., Ferd., Pros., Alonso.

What is't? a spirit?
Lord, how it looks about. Believe me, sir,
It carries a brave form.

I.ii.413.

Pros., Mir., Ferd.

Shakespeare: an active approach

1 • *Coriolanus: Freeze Frames*

We must suggest the people in what hatred
He still hath held them.

II.i.243.

Brutus, Sic.

I'll not over the threshold till my lord return
from the wars.

I.iii.74.

Virg., Vol., Val.

if thou wilt have
The leading of thine own revenges, take
Th'one half of my commission.

IV.v.137.

Auf., Cor.

in the name of the people,
And in the power of us the tribunes, we
Ev'n from this instant, banish him our city.

III.iii.99.

Sic., Brut., Com., Cor., Plebeians.

Go, get you home, you fragments!

I.i.221.

Cor., Men., Citizens.

Ay, Martius, Caius Martius, dost thou think
I'll grace thee with that robbery, thy stolen
name,
Coriolanus, in Corioles?

V.vi.88.

Auf., Cor., Commoners.

Wife, mother, child, I know not. My affairs
Are servanted to others.

V.ii.80.

Cor., Men., Auf.

O mother, mother!
What have you done?

V.iii.182.

Cor., Vol., Virg., Son, Auf.

1 • Hamlet: Freeze Frames

Horatio, thou art e'en as just a man
As e'er my conversation coped withal.

III.ii.48.

Hamlet and Horatio.

Were you not sent for? Is it your own inclining?

II.ii.269.

Hamlet, Ros., Guild.

Revenge his foul and most unnatural murder.

I.v.24.

Ghost, Hamlet.

And for that purpose I'll anoint my sword.

IV.vii.139.

Laert., Claud.

You need not tell us what Lord Hamlet said:
We heard it all.

III.i.176.

Pol. Oph. Claud.

You shall do marvellous wisely, good Reynaldo,
Before you visit him, to make inquire
Of his behaviour,

II.i.3.

Pol., Reyn.

Look here upon this picture, and on this.

III.iv.53.

Hamlet, Gertrude.

Where's your father?

III.i.129.

Hamlet, Oph., Pol., Claud.

Shakespeare: an active approach

2 • *Kaleidoscope*

FOCUS ON: INTRODUCTION TO SHAKESPEARE'S LANGUAGE

SMALL GROUP ACTIVITY

KNOWLEDGE OF PLAY NOT REQUIRED

Procedure

For this you will need a number of cards, each with a different phrase or line from the text on it; you should choose ones which do not contain references to specific places or characters.

Give these out, one to each student, and ask them to spend a little while exploring all the possible meanings of their phrase and the ways in which it could be delivered, trying it out to themselves.

Now divide the class into groups of about four; the task is to use their lines to create a short scene, with any setting or any characters they like (not those from within the play) as though it were an extract from some unknown play.

Lines may be spoken by any member of the group and as many times as they like; pauses and silent actions may be used to expand the 'extract', but only a minimum of additional words may be inserted, to link phrases as necessary.

The result should make some sort of sense — as though it really were a fragment of another play.

This exercise obviously doesn't help with understanding of the play to be studied but it does make Shakespeare's language seem a little less formidable to those who are unfamiliar with it.

Examples

The Student's Notes provide a set of cards for ANTONY AND CLEOPATRA. Below are examples from HAMLET and CORIOLANUS.

From HAMLET:

He is the card or calendar of gentry.
Report me and my cause aright to the unsatisfied.
Diseases desperate grown, by desperate appliance are relieved, or not at all.
Have you heard the argument? Is there no offence in it?
Thou know'st 'tis common, all that lives must die.
Thou wretched, rash intruding fool, farewell.
Indeed, my lord, you made me believe so.
Good gentlemen, he hath much talked of you.
O horrible! O horrible, most horrible!
You go not till I set you up a glass where you may see the inmost part of you.
I have sent to seek him and to find the body.
I will speak daggers to her, but use none.
Thy commandment all alone shall live within the book and volume of my brain.
My spirits grow dull and fain I would beguile the tedious day with sleep.
Why, this is hire and salary, not revenge.

From CORIOLANUS:

He loved his mother dearly.
Sir, if you'd save your life, fly to your house.
Come, come, you have been too rough, something too rough.
You souls of geese that bear the shapes of men, how have you run from slaves that apes would beat,
Nay, but speak not maliciously.
What he cannot help in his nature, you account a vice in him.
He is grown too proud to be so valian.
Our arm's in the field,
Hark, our drums are bringing forth our youth.
They fear us not, but issue forth their city.
I thank you general; but cannot make my heart consent to take a bribe to pay my sword.
I request you to give my poor host freedom.
Nature teaches beasts to know their friends.
He has spoken like a traitor and shall answer as traitors do.
Consider you what services he has done for his country?

Follow-up

On to the play itself!

2 • Kaleidoscope: Antony and Cleopatra

Tell him he wears the rose of youth upon him.

He fishes, drinks and wastes the lamps of night in revel.

I could have given less matter a better ear.

My salad days, when I was green in judgement, cold in blood, to say as I said then.

The long day's task is done and we must sleep.

His soldiership is twice the other twain.

Eternity was in our lips and eyes, bliss in our brows' bent.

She is cunning past man's thought.

Come, let's have one other gaudy night.

Why, sir, give the gods a thankful sacrifice.

Women are not in their best fortunes strong.

Come, we have no friend but resolution and the briefest end.

Ay me, most wretched, that have my heart parted betwixt two friends.

The odds are gone and there is nothing left remarkable beneath the visiting moon.

I have done ill, of which I do accuse myself so sorely, that I will joy no more.

Let him not leave out the colour of her hair. Bring me word quickly.

3 • *Question and Answer*

FOCUS ON: GENERAL UNDERSTANDING/REVISION
WHOLE CLASS ACTIVITY
KNOWLEDGE OF PLAY REQUIRED

Procedure

Find a series of questions and answers from within a play, enough for each student to be given one question *or* one answer. Write each on a separate card, shuffle them, and deal them out to a circle of students. Each one must now find the other half of his/her pair, by moving round the group, but must say nothing except the words on the card.

When question and answer are reunited, the pair try to identify who they are and the circumstances in which the lines were delivered in the play. Students now reassemble in a circle, but in pairs, and the question and answer are delivered in turn, for the group to identify.

From MACBETH
But who did bid thee join with us?
Stands Scotland where it did?
Is't far you ride?

How came she by that light?
Dismayed not this our captains, Macbeth and Banquo?
How does my wife?
What, quite unmanned in folly?
What is't you do?
What's to be done?
Wherefore was that cry?
From KING LEAR:
Can you make no use of nothing, Nuncle?
What is your study?
Wherefore to Dover?

But have I fallen, or no?
What's he that speaks for Edmund, Earl of Gloucester?
Who dead, speak man?

Upon the crown of the cliff, what thing was that which parted from you?
How fares your majesty?
Where's my Fool? I have not seen him these two days.

What need one?

This makes a good 'warm-up' for some further dramatic exploration of the play, but is equally valuable as a revision exercise.

Examples

The Students' Notes offer a set of cards for THE TEMPEST; there are examples from KING LEAR and MACBETH below.

Follow-up

General discussion of character, relationships and plot.

Macbeth
Alas poor country, almost afraid to know itself.
As far, my lord, as will fill up the time 'twixt this and supper.
Why, it stood by her.
Yes, as sparrows eagles, or the hare the lion.
Why, well.
If I stand here, I saw him.
A deed without a name.
Be innocent of the knowledge, dearest chuck.
The queen, my lord, is dead.

Why, no boy, nothing can be made out of nothing.
How to prevent the fiend and to kill vermin.
Because I would not see thy cruel nails pluck out his poor old eyes.
From the dread summit of this chalky bourn.
Himself.
Your lady, sir, your lady: and her sister by her is poisoned.
A poor unfortunate beggar.

You do me wrong to take me out o' th' grave.
Since my young lady's going into France, sir, the Fool hath much pined away.
O reason not the need!

                    TEACHER'S NOTES

3 • Question and Answer: The Tempest

How now, moody, what is't thou canst demand?

My liberty.

Wherefore did they not that hour destroy us?

Well demanded, wench, my tale provokes that question.

But how should Prospero be living and be here?

First, noble friend, let me embrace your age, whose honour cannot be measured or confined.

Dost thou hear?

Your tale, sir, would cure deafness.

How shall this be compassed? Canst thou bring me to the party?

Yea, yea, my lord; I'll yield him thee asleep.

I'th' name of something holy, sir, why stand you in this strange stare?

O it is monstrous, monstrous! Methought the billows spoke and told me of it.

But are they, Ariel, safe?

Not a hair perished: on their sustaining garments not a blemish, but fresher than before.

My prime request, which I do last pronounce is, O you wonder, if you be maid or no?

No wonder, sir, but certainly a maid.

Shakespeare: an active approach

4 • *A Shakespeare Journal*

FOCUS ON: PERSONAL RESPONSE

INDIVIDUAL WORK

KNOWLEDGE OF PLAY NOT REQUIRED

Procedure

Before beginning study of a Shakespeare play for A-level, issue each student with an exercise book, not for taking notes (though some notes may find their way into it) but for recording their personal responses to reading the play and to the various activities undertaken in exploring it.

Encourage them to record their reactions to each scene or act read, after the lesson is over, and to note down a line or two that seemed to them particularly effective.

Visits to the theatre can produce reviews, as can watching a video of the play, where interpretations of character by director and actor can provoke comment.

Some students may also wish to include examples of their own creative work stimulated by the ideas or images of the play, perhaps in the form of poems or short stories.

After a suitable interval, take the exercise books in to have a look at them (unless any student feels that it is a purely private journal) and try to find comments to make, without, of course, any corrections or grades. It's essential that students don't feel their journal is like an essay to be marked, but rather a record of opinions and ideas which can be shared with you.

Other examples

There are a number of poems which have been written as a response to a Shakespeare play; T.S.Eliot's 'Marina', for instance, is a marvellous evocation of the 'stream of consciousness' in Pericles' mind as he, at first incredulously, realises that his daughter is alive and breathing.

To read something like this with them will widen their view of what sort of response is appropriate. It certainly does not have to be a conventional 'lit-crit' essay, and some A-Level Boards are now including a creative option in coursework elements. Exploring feelings and ideas, without worrying about textual evidence for once, can be refreshing and often helpful in the long run to the more usual sort of question.

Follow-up

Wall displays (with the writer's permission) of poems, interpretations, reviews of productions, both from newspapers and from students, and even pictures, drawn and painted as a result of their contact with a play, make a stimulating environment for class discussion.

4 • A Shakespeare Journal

FOCUS ON: PERSONAL RESPONSE

Example

After reading Act I i and ii of HAMLET:

> I think I would be rather like the Elizabethans with regard to the union of Gertrude and Claudius and see it as incest; their marriage must be tainted by the death of the old Hamlet. The King himself admits it when he says "with mirth in funeral and with dirge in marriage." I thought immediately that he had married for his own gain. I ask myself why G. should have agreed to marry her former brother-in-law so soon after her husband's death? It must imply that she was not fond of the latter. I do not blame Hamlet for how he is towards them – he is pert, rude and intense – but I can understand why. I am trying to keep an open mind, however!

From a later entry:

> We were given an extract from a speech, so that we each had a segment, but disjointed. This time we had people up in the gallery and below. The last person to speak was in the central spotlight and we all decided to speak in stage whispers, which was quite effective. As each line was spoken we pointed by the one in the centre, without looking at him, because we were his thoughts. I felt this was very dramatic and it made me feel really part of the play itself, instead of being on the outside.

Activity

These extracts are from a Shakespeare Journal kept by a student just beginning her study of HAMLET for A-Level. You may well be taking notes during some of your lessons on your Shakespeare play but there is a lot to be gained from a slightly different approach, as you begin on a set play.

Try to record a few lines about your personal reaction to each lesson, or to each Act or scene you read on your own. Even if these only take the form of questions which puzzle you, they can be useful to remind you what to ask your teacher, or what to turn back to when you have read further on and understood a bit more.

Note down, too, any powerful lines which strike you as memorable; you will in this way begin to build up a fund of 'evidence' for future essays.

If you go to see a production in the theatre, or watch a video, take some time to jot down reactions and opinions and add, if you like, reviews cut out of newspapers to compare with your own.

Follow-up

Add to these entries any creative and imaginative pieces that the play stimulates you to write. Perhaps you might imagine the thoughts of a character at a certain point in the play – like a soliloquy that Shakespeare didn't write – or a bit of dialogue which takes place off stage. Your own poems and stories on themes found in the play are also a valuable way of exploring the imaginative world of the play.

You need not show your journal to anyone else if you would prefer not to.

5 • *Creative Responses*

FOCUS ON: PERSONAL RESPONSE

INDIVIDUAL WORK

KNOWLEDGE OF PLAY REQUIRED

Procedure

More and more examination boards are introducing optional coursework elements into A-Level syllabuses and in some of these there is the possibility of a creative response from the students. It seems a natural development from the kind of work done at GCSE, and can provide an imaginative student with the opportunity of demonstrating understanding of the text at the same time as individual response. Even when there is no such chance to include it in the coursework, the actual process is valuable to an understanding of the play.

Some ideas for writing are included in the students' notes but these are not, of course, exhaustive. They will probably come up with a great many more in the course of discussion.

Examples

1 **Your own soliloquy:** from HAMLET: Ophelia's thoughts as she awaits Hamlet's arrival in Act III i, knowing that her father and Claudius are hidden within earshot.

from MACBETH: Banquo's thoughts at the end of the scene in which Duncan's body has been discovered, Act II.iii.

2 **Diary entries:** from KING LEAR: Kent's diary entry after he leaves Lear's court.

from ANTONY AND CLEOPATRA: Enobarbus's diary after Antony has agreed to the marriage with Octavia.

3 **Letters:** from THE TEMPEST: the letter Ferdinand might have written, to put in a bottle, after falling in love with Miranda.

from ANTONY AND CLEOPATRA: Octavia's letter to Antony imploring him to make peace with Caesar and return to Rome.

4 **Off-stage:** from HAMLET: The conversation between Rosencrantz and Guildenstern after they have been employed by Claudius and Gertrude to find out what is wrong with Hamlet (with apologies to Tom Stoppard!).

from CORIOLANUS: the conversation between Menenius and Volumnia before she goes to beg mercy for Rome from her son.

Follow-up

Some of these will certainly be worth reading aloud to the group and would lead to useful discussion, especially if interpretations have to be supported by reference to the text.

5 • Creative Responses

FOCUS ON: PERSONAL RESPONSE

Examples

1 Write your own soliloquy: Find a moment in the play when it would seem useful to explore a character's state of mind – one where Shakespeare has not supplied us with a soliloquy – and write your own version as an interior monologue. This could be in prose, or in blank verse if you are brave enough; the important thing is to think yourself into the character and see things through his/her eyes.

2 Letters: These give an opportunity to reveal what someone is thinking about what is going on around him or her, with the added dimension of a particular audience to direct it at.

3 Diary: We all confide to our diaries things we would not admit even to our friends.

4 'Off-stage': Try writing one of the scenes Shakespeare does not show us – the ones that happen off-stage and are perhaps reported to us. Choose one such incident and script the dialogue.

Activity

Choose one of these, or any other imaginative piece which the play suggests to you; try to choose a style that suits the character and the sort of vocabulary he/she might use (or its contemporary equivalent).

Follow-up

You could collect together the creative items and edit them into a booklet to be photocopied and distributed, or you could create a wall display, to share ideas.

Polonius – Interior Monologue at beginning of play.

Good old King Hamlet slain, and no more than two portions of an Annum passed; his Queen, married with his brother, rules this sorry State, much to the disgust of my noble lord Hamlet, whom, it must be said, considers his highness with barely concealed contempt, indeed may I venture – stripped to a bare Bodkin? Such insolence upon the part of my lord has unfortunately disrupted the harmonic surface of the newly found court, and now serious observations concerning the Prince's sanity are of paramount importance, for, it must be my devoted duty to protect the safety and interests of my truly regal ruler, to whom I am so indebted; then I may be struck from this court in which I hold the position of Chief Councillor.

From Hamlet's diary – set down immediately after seeing his father's ghost

The first time I saw it, it struck a cold chill in my heart, its grey cold features bearing a striking resemblance to my late father. It fixed me with its piercing eyes, it was as though they were seeing right into my very soul and beckoned slowly. Transfixed by horror but also by curiosity, I followed obediently, finding myself unable to disobey. It glided silently before me through the stormy night, then, turning, again directed that piercingly cold stare at me. The pale grey lips parted in readiness to speak and I waited in fearful anticipation of what was to come …

6 • *Thinking Visually*

FOCUS ON: PLOT/RELATIONSHIPS

INDIVIDUAL OR PAIR WORK

KNOWLEDGE OF PLAY REQUIRED

Procedure

Visual aids to memory can be very useful, and the process of presenting information in diagrammatic form helps students to focus on essentials and to look for their own textual evidence.

The example below shows a 'spider' diagram to indicate Hamlet's relationship with each of the other main characters: the quotations were chosen by students to crystallise, in one phrase, the feelings Hamlet has about each of them.

A reverse of the same exercise would have the arrows pointing the other way and the quotations would then be *from* each character about or to Hamlet.

Follow-up

There are plenty of other ways of presenting ideas in a visual form:

1 The play's plot as a continuous line winding across the page, with points of crisis and the passage of time marked on it. This can be a good way of looking at a complex political plot, like ANTONY AND CLEOPATRA.

2 Triangles: the points are characters, the lines joining them are composed of quotations symbolising the relationships.

3 Columns: headed with names of characters and a series of questions down the left-hand margin to point parallels and contrasts (e.g. Hamlet, Laertes and Fortinbras). Short quotations are used to answer the questions.

Diagrams can be shared by wall display or by photocopying and distributing.

Example

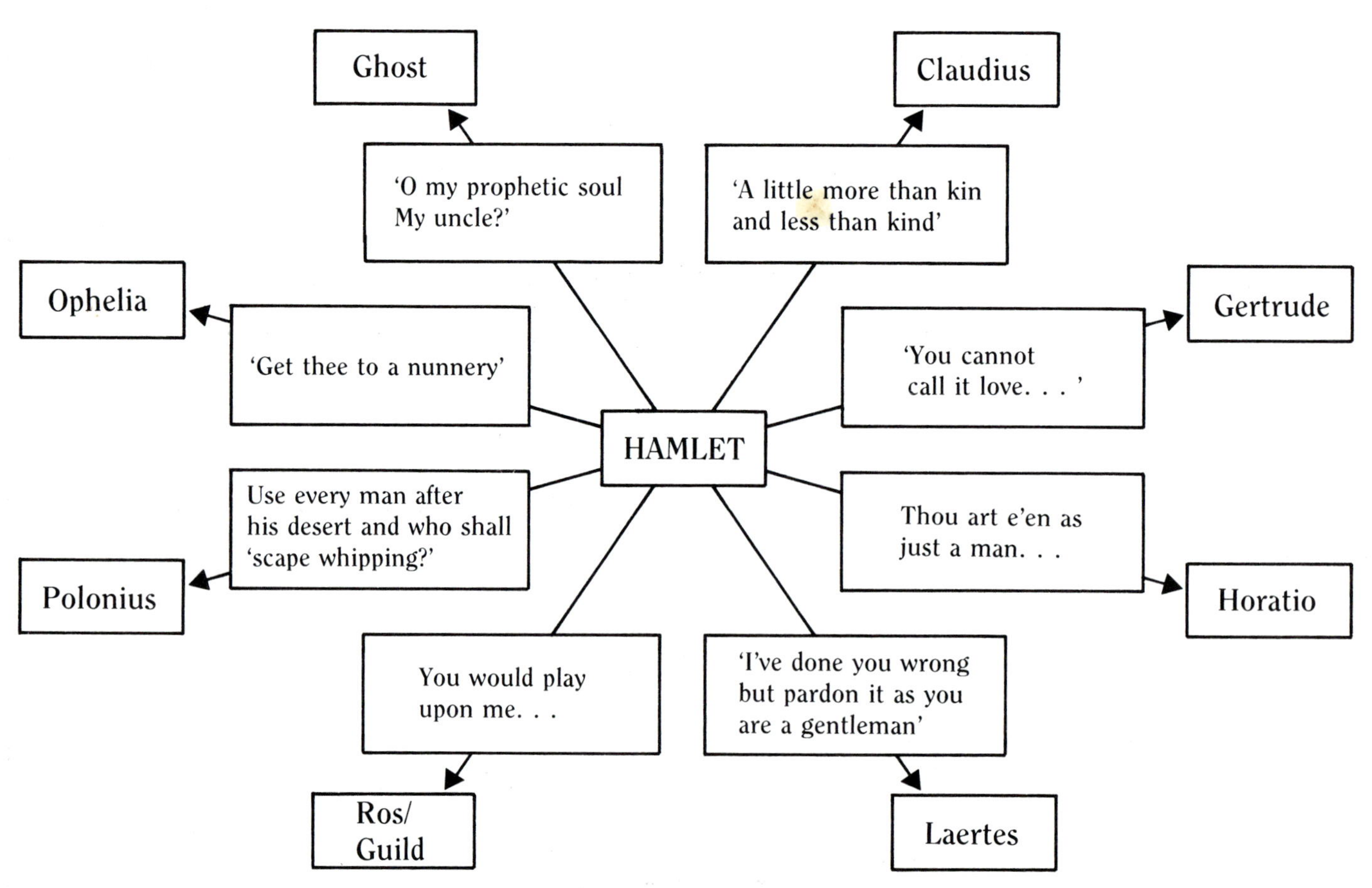

6 • *Thinking Visually*

FOCUS ON: PLOT/RELATIONSHIPS

Example

It is far easier to remember things if you can impress them on your mind by a visual diagram, and, if you can call up a short quotation to sum up an idea, it will often bring a whole lot of other points along with it.

Activity

Write the name of an important character (A) in the central box, and eight other characters who are connected with A at the arrow points. Now find your own short quotations which seem to sum up A's attitude to each character, and write them in the boxes on the connecting lines.

Then copy the diagram with the arrows *reversed,* and use phrases from the play to show what each thinks and feels about A.

Follow-up

Experiment with other ways of presenting information visually. Try a time chart of the plot/s, or draw a diagram of events arranged as a board game, or perhaps a Venn diagram of relationships. Whenever you can, use short quotations instead of your own words.

Don't all do the same kind of visual presentations and, when you have finished, share your presentation with everyone in the class.

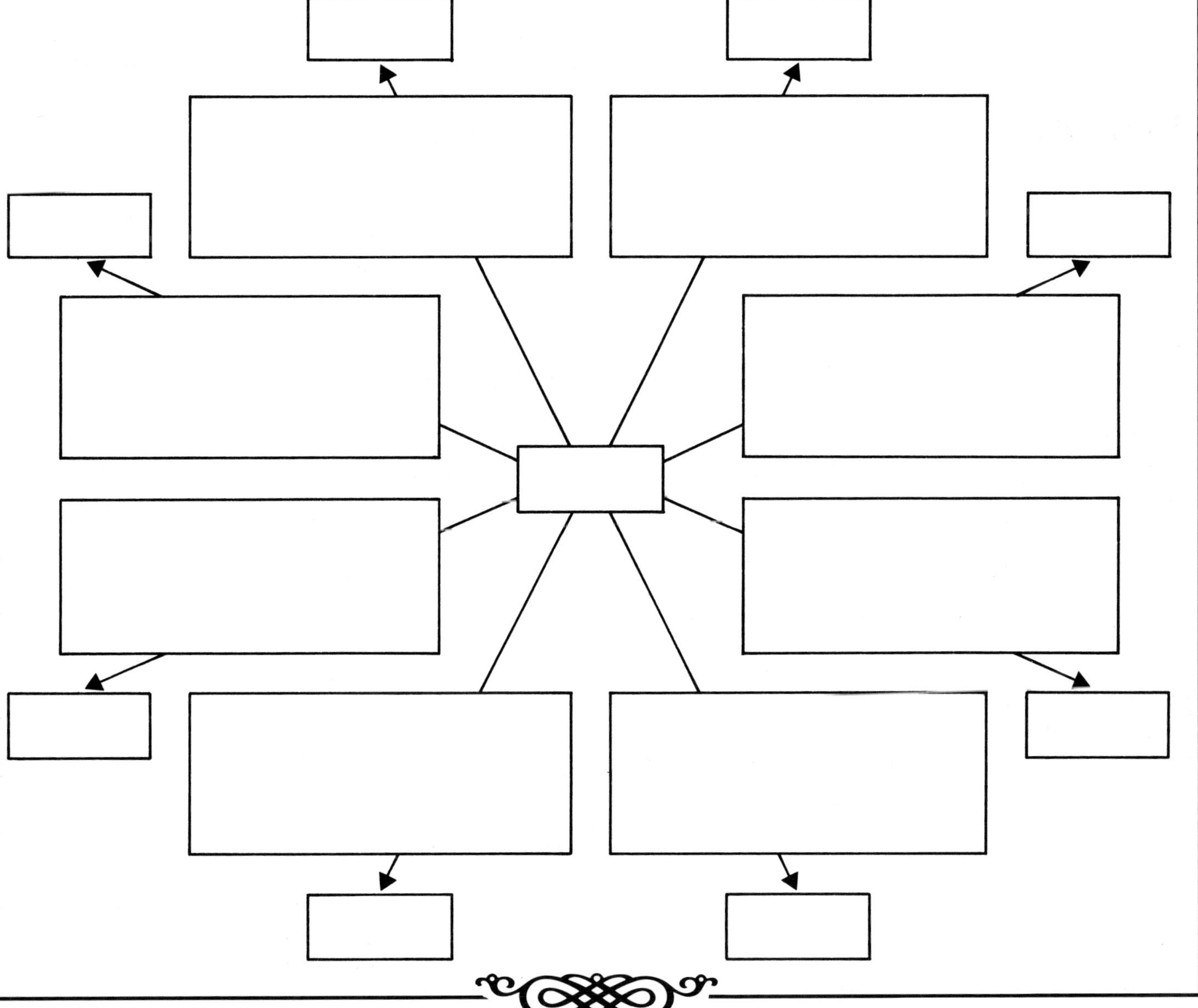

7 • *Dreams*

FOCUS ON: CHARACTER

GROUP WORK

KNOWLEDGE OF PLAY REQUIRED

Procedure

This exercise can be useful after a first reading and before embarking on essay work on the main characters, or can be used as a revision exercise.

Divide the class into groups of three or four and allocate a different character to each group. Names could be written on cards, for each group to draw one at random.

Then issue the instructions in the Students' Notes and leave them to it. They will have to search through the play for material, as well as devise their presentation, so allow at least an hour for this exercise.

Examples

The idea will work with any play but tends to have more scope if the character is seen to be suffering from a sense of guilt, or is faced with a dilemma and the need to choose a course of action.

1 From CORIOLANUS: before he has to decide whether to destroy Rome or not.

2 From MACBETH: Macbeth himself, the night before the final battle at Dunsinane. (This is probably the one which parallels most closely the model from RICHARD III.)

3 From HAMLET: Laertes, before the last Act and after plotting with Claudius; Gertrude after the 'Closet' scene.

4 From KING LEAR: Edmund, before his death.

Follow-up

Discussion of each presentation is clearly as important as performing the scenes themselves, and should centre on whether the chosen lines symbolised successfully the dilemma or guilt.

Essay work on the chosen characters could follow, and would benefit from the search for evidence in the text which this exercise involves.

7 • *Dreams*

FOCUS ON: CHARACTER

Examples

Shakespeare sometimes used the device of a dream to present a state of mind. In JULIUS CAESAR, Brutus, on the eve of the Battle of Philippi, sees the ghost of Julius Caesar in his dream: through this the audience can share in his sense of guilt and the ominous foreboding he feels about the impending battle.

In the example below, from RICHARD III, each of Richard's victims appears to him in a dream before the Battle of Bosworth and accuses him, as well as wishing his opponent, Richmond, good fortune.

The Ghost of Lord Hastings appears

Ghost [to Richard]: Bloody and guilty, guiltily awake,
  And in a bloody battle end thy days
  Think on Lord Hastings: despair, and die!
[to Richmond] Quiet untroubled soul, awake, awake!
  Arm, fight, and conquer, for fair England's sake!
[vanishes

The Ghosts of the two young Princes appear

Ghosts *[to Richard]:* Dream on thy cousins smotheréd
  in the Tower:
Let us be lead within thy bosom, Richard,
And weigh thee down to ruin, shame, and death!
Thy nephews' souls bid thee despair and die!
[to Richmond] Sleep, Richmond, sleep in peace, and
  wake in joy;
Good angels guard thee from the boar's annoy!
Live, and beget a happy race of kings!
Edward's unhappy sons do bid thee flourish.
[they vanish

The Ghost of Anne his wife appears

Ghost *[to Richard]* Richard, thy wife, that wretched
  Anne thy wife,
That never slept a quiet hour with thee,
Now fills thy sleep with perturbations:
To-morrow in the battle think on me,
And fall thy edgeless sword: despair, and die!
[to Richmond] Thou quiet soul, sleep thou a quiet sleep:

Dream of success and happy victory!
Thy adversary's wife doth pray for thee.
[vanishes

The Ghost of Buckingham appears

Ghost [to Richard]: The first was I that helped thee to
  the crown;
The last was I that felt thy tyranny:
O, in the battle think on Buckingham,
And die in terror of thy guiltiness!
Dream on, dream on, of bloody deeds and death:
Fainting, despair; despairing, yield thy breath!
[to Richmond] I died for hope ere I could lend thee aid:
But cheer thy heart, and be thou not dismayed:
God and good angels fight on Richmond's side;
And Richard falls in height of all his pride.
[vanishes

Activity

When your group has been given a character to work on, devise a dream he/she might have, immediately before or after a crucial moment in the play. Other characters may appear to remind him or her of earlier events, of words spoken, of promises broken, etc.

Your only restriction is that you may only use words and speeches from the play (though you could also have silent accusers), with the minimum of your own words to link them where necessary.

Now decide how to present this dream in dramatic form – movements, echoes, voices over, chanting, etc., – to show the state of mind.

Follow-up

Because this makes you look in the text for suitable lines it is a very good preparation for essay work on character. Even if you are not immediately writing this kind of essay, take time to make some notes and to collect some of the quotations before you forget them.

 Shakespeare: an active approach

8 • *Student as Director*

FOCUS ON: CHARACTER INTERPRETATION

SMALL GROUP ACTIVITY

KNOWLEDGE OF PLAY REQUIRED

Procedure

The purpose of the exercise is to illustrate how the script of a play is often capable of more than one interpretation; there is no definitive performance of Polonius, any more than of Hamlet himself.

Give small groups the piece of text to read and to discuss briefly: the Students' Notes suggest two possible interpretations of Polonius and you could ask half the groups to follow one and the other half the other.

A good way to get them started would be to ask them to improvise the scenes in their own words first — not for performance but to help them to find suitable moves and gestures in 'rehearsal'.

The outcome should be at least one presentation of each interpretation, followed by general discussion of how far the text supports the views of Polonius seen here.

Examples from other plays

I From ANTONY AND CLEOPATRA: Octavius Caesar: is he a fond and loving brother or a calculating politician, using his sister as a means of knowingly creating an alliance which already contains the seeds of future convenient discord?

2 From MACBETH: Banquo: is he prepared to keep silent because of self interest, or the prospects of his son? Or is he an essentially good man (contrasted with Macbeth) who is biding his time until he can join the rebels and overthrow Macbeth?

Follow-up

Ask students to write Director's Notes for the actors in the scene, or to annotate the script with these directions.

Other scenes from HAMLET can be given to different groups, e.g. Ophelia in III.i.90: does she agree to act as bait to help Hamlet, or out of fear of her father?

Written work can follow on Polonius; perhaps the 'justice' of his death e.g. 'Did Polonius deserve to die?'

8 • *Student as Director*

FOCUS ON: CHARACTER INTERPRETATION

Example

Polonius   What is't Ophelia he hath said to you.?
Ophelia   So please you, something touching the
 Lord Hamlet.
Polonius   Marry well bethought.
 'Tis told me he hath very oft of late
 Given private time to you, and you yourself
 Have of your audience been most free and
  bounteous.
 If it be so, as so 'tis put on me,
 And that in way of caution, I must tell you,
 You do not understand yourself so clearly
 As it behoves my daughter, and your honour.
 What is between you? Give me up the truth.
Ophelia   He hath my lord of late made many
 tenders
 Of his affection to me.
Polonius   Affection? Pooh, you speak like a green
 girl
 Unsifted in such perilous circumstance.
 Do you believe his tenders as you call them?
Ophelia   I do not know my lord what I should
 think.
Polonius   Marry I'll teach you; think yourself a
 baby,
 That you have ta'en these tenders for true pay
 Which are not sterling. Tender yourself more
  dearly;
 Or – not to crack the wind of the poor phrase
 Running it thus – you'll tender me a fool.
Ophelia   My lord he hath importuned me with
 love
 In honourable fashion.
Polonius   Ay, fashion you may call it; go to, go to.
Ophelia   And hath given countenance to his speech,
 my lord,
With almost all the holy vows of heaven.
Polonius   Ay, springes to catch woodcocks. I do know,
 When the blood burns, how prodigal the soul
 Lends the tongue vows. These blazes daughter,
 Giving more light than heat, extinct in both,
 Even in their promise, as it is a-making,
 You must not take for fire. From this time
 Be somewhat scanter of your maiden presence.
 Set your entreatments at a higher rate
 Than a command to parley. For Lord Hamlet,
 Believe so much in him that he is young,

And with a larger tether may he walk
Than may be given you. In few Ophelia,
Do not believe his vows, for they are brokers,
Not of that dye which their investments show,
Be mere implorators of unholy suits,
Breathing like sanctified and pious bonds
The better to beguile. This is for all:
I would not in plain terms from this time forth
Have you so slander any moment leisure
As to give words or talk with the Lord Hamlet.
Look to't I charge you; come your ways.
Ophelia   I shall obey, my lord.

from Act I.iii.

Activity

Working in small groups, read this piece of dialogue through and discuss how the character of Polonius should be played.

Is he a concerned and loving parent, anxious that his only daughter should not be hurt, or is he an authoritarian father, perhaps even bullying? A recent touring production of the R.S.C. took the latter view and even had him striking her across the face at one point.

You may well think that the best performance would be one between the two extremes but, for this activity, half of you should take on one interpretation and half the other, and work out voice-expression, gestures and movements which emphasise your given view.

Share your presentation with the rest of the class as a rehearsed reading, with movement.

Follow-up

Look closely at how Polonius' character appears elsewhere in the play. What are the consequences of your interpretation for other scenes in which he appears? What would be his tone of voice, for instance, in the lines: 'you need not tell us what Lord Hamlet said,/We heard it all.'?

Our understanding of the play depends a lot on which way we see his character. For example, what is his relationship with Claudius in Act II.ii? Has he switched allegiance from the old Hamlet or was he always Claudius's man? And what about the Reynaldo scene? What are his motives here? (II.i.).

   Shakespeare: an active approach   **25**

9 • *Madness*

FOCUS ON: OPHELIA

PAIR WORK

KNOWLEDGE OF PLAY REQUIRED

Procedure

The activity is concentrated on Ophelia and all the factors that contribute to her madness. Starting with the 'mad scenes', students work in pairs backwards and trace what factors and people have brought her to this situation. You can ask each pair to cover all the points, or give each pair a different thread to follow.

1 Grief for her father – looking at earlier scenes with Polonius.

2 Love for Hamlet – her account of his meeting with her with his doublet all unbraced, and all scenes where they are together.

3 Relationship with Laertes – advice before departure for Paris, and present distress at her madness.

4 What she has seen happen at Court – see below.

This material could be presented as an illustrated talk, with comments interspersed with quotations.

Example

The flowers and herbs she distributes in this scene could perhaps be clues to the fact that she has noticed more of what has been going on than is usually suggested. It is interesting to think for whom each herb is intended; perhaps fennel (for flattery) and columbines (for ingratitude) are given to Claudius, and the daisy (for deceit) either to him or to Gertrude? If so, surely these suggest she has observed signs of their adultery? It may be that she understands more of Hamlet's situation than he thinks.

A recent London production had her on stage through a number of the earlier scenes when the stage directions do not mention her, thus emphasising her role as observer.

Follow-up

This would make a good lead-in to written work on Ophelia, or could result in an improvised role-play of a case conference between a psychiatrist, doctor and interested parties to discuss Ophelia's state of mind. (see unit on Case Conference: KING LEAR.)

9 • *Madness*

FOCUS ON: OPHELIA

Example

Enter Gentleman *with* Ophelia

Ophelia   Where is the beauteous majesty of Denmark?
Queen   How now Ophelia!
Ophelia   [*Sings*]   How should I your true love know
                    From another one?
                    By his cockle hat and staff,
                    And his sandal shoon.
Queen   Alas sweet lady, what imports this song?
Ophelia   Say you? Nay, pray you mark
        [*Sings*]   He is dead and gone lady
                    He is dead and gone,
                    At this head a grass-green turf,
                    At his heels a stone.
                Oho!
Queen   Nay but Ophelia, –
Ophelia   Pray you mark.
     [*Sings*]   White his shroud as the mountain snow –

Enter KING

Queen   Alas, look here my lord.
Ophelia   [*Sings*]   Larded all with sweet flowers,
                    Which bewept to the grave did not go
                    With true-love showers.
King   How do you pretty lady?
Ophelia   Well, God dild you. They say the owl was a
    baker's daughter. Lord, we know what we are, but
    know not what we may be. God be at your table.
King   Conceit upon her father.
Ophelia   Pray let's have no words of this, but when they
    ask you what it means, say you this:
    [*Sings*]   Tomorrow is Saint Valentine's day,
                All in the morning betime,
                And I maid at your window,
                        To be your Valentine.
                Then up he rose, and donned his clothes,
                And dupped the chamber door,
                Let in the maid, that out a maid,
                        Never departed more.
King   Pretty Ophelia.
Ophelia   Indeed without an oath I'll make an end on't.
                By Gis and by Saint Charity,
                Alack and fie for shame,
                Young men will do't if they come to't,
                By Cock, they are to blame.
                Quoth she, before you tumbled me,
                        You promised me to wed.

He answers,
            So would I'a done by yonder sun,
            an thou hadst not come to my bed.
King   How long hath she been thus?
Ophelia   I hope all will be well. We must be patient, but I
    cannot choose but weep to think they should lay him
    i' th' cold ground. My brother shall know of it, and so
    I thank you for your good counsel. Come, my coach.
    Good night ladies, good night, sweet ladies, good
    night, good night.   [*Exit*
King   Follow her close; give her good watch I pray you.
                                        [*Exit Horatio*

from Act IV.v.

Read this through carefully and look also at the second of Ophelia's mad scenes in Act IV.v., when Laertes is present, from line 151 to 195.

Activity

Try to isolate in these two extracts any clues as to what has led to Ophelia's present madness. Consider signs of grief at her father's death, her rejection by Hamlet, what she has seen and heard in the Court and any other factors you think could be relevant.

Now discuss any earlier speeches, scenes and relationships which might offer any other insights into her state of mind at this time. Look at

- Laertes' advice to her, Act I.iii.1–51.
- Polonius' advice in same scene, 88–136.
- Her account of the encounter with Hamlet, Act II.i.75–98.
- The plot to overhear her and Hamlet together, Act III.i.44 to end.
- Play scene : Hamlet's comments to her, especially Act III.ii. 100–239

Follow-up

Use the material you have collected to write:
Either a commentary on the relationship between Hamlet and Ophelia,
Or an interior monologue of Ophelia's thoughts while waiting for Hamlet (III.i.42–89).

   Shakespeare: an active approach

10 • *Modern Dress Production*

FOCUS ON: THEATRE

GROUP WORK: IN FOURS

KNOWLEDGE OF PLAY REQUIRED

Procedure

The purpose of the activity is to show how modern dress can bring out aspects of the text not otherwise evident, and can make us see some scenes with new eyes.

First ask the students to rehearse a prepared reading of the given scene according to the instructions in their notes, and to 'stage' it with moves and actions as far as the available space will allow.

Discussion will follow of how this interpretation modifies our views of (a) Claudius and (b) Rosencrantz and Guildenstern. Ask them to find evidence from elsewhere in the play to justify such a reading and also anything they feel conflicts with it.

Now they should think through a complete modern dress version of the play and focus on which scenes will present problems and which will benefit from a contemporary setting.

Other examples

Most plays will lend themselves to such a discussion. A National Theatre production of CORIOLANUS a few years ago emphasised the director's dilemma – modern dress was effective in directing attention to the universal quality of the play as it forced us to apply the situations to contemporary life, but 'suspension of disbelief' was strained by the existence of guns which were never used at any important juncture – particularly in the death of Coriolanus, when it was felt that they would have been.

ANTONY AND CLEOPATRA produces similar problems of weapons and suicides, but a Caesar seen as an unscrupulous modern politician may offer new insights.

The intention of all these questions is of course to send them back to the play itself for evidence and justification, as well as to shed new light on character.

Follow-up

This could be a good way into a piece of work on Claudius, or an examination of Rosencrantz and Guildenstern and their relationship with Hamlet.

TEACHER'S NOTES

10 • *Modern Dress Production*

FOCUS ON: THEATRE

Example

King Now Hamlet, where's Polonius?

Hamlet At supper.

King At supper? Where?

Hamlet Not where he eats, but where 'a is eaten; a certain convocation of politic worms are e'en at him. Your worm is your only emperor for diet; we fat all creatures else to fat us, and we fat ourselves for maggots; your fat king and your lean beggar is but variable service, two dishes, but to one table – that's the end.

King Alas, alas!

Hamlet A man may fish with the worm that hath eat of a king, and eat of the fish that hath fed of that worm.

King What dost thou mean by this?

Hamlet Nothing but to show you how a king may go a progress through the guts of a beggar.

King Where is Polonius?

Hamlet In heaven. Send thither to see; if your messenger find him not there, seek him i' th' other place yourself. But if indeed you find him not within this month, you shall nose him as you go up the stairs into the lobby.

King Go seek him there.

[To some Attendants

Hamlet 'A will stay till you come.

[Exeunt Attendants

King Hamlet, this deed, for thine especial safety—
Which we do tender, as we dearly grieve
For that which thou hast done—must send thee hence
With fiery quickness. Therefore prepare thyself.
The bark is ready, and the wind at help,
Th' associates tend, and every thing is bent
For England.

Hamlet For England.

King Ay Hamlet.

Hamlet Good.

King So is it if thou knew'st our purposes.

Hamlet I see a cherub that sees them. But come, for England. Farewell dear mother.

King Thy loving father, Hamlet.

Hamlet My mother – father and mother is man and wife, man and wife is one flesh; and so, my mother. Come, for England. *[Exit*

from Act IV.iii.

Activity

Re-read this dialogue in your groups and remind yourselves at what point in the play it occurs.

Now imagine the director has decided on a **modern dress production** of HAMLET and has seen Claudius as a kind of modern dictator – a military despot whose coup has ousted the young Hamlet from his rightful inheritance, and who is surrounded by his strong-arm henchmen, among whom are Rosencrantz and Guildenstern.

How will these points influence the performance of this scene? When Hamlet is brought in, is he dragged? The dialogue could take on a new and sinister note if seen as an interrogation (lights shining in his eyes perhaps? open violence?).

Prepare a rehearsed reading of this extract, with action and movement to bring out such a view.

Follow-up

Extend the idea of a modern-dress HAMLET to the rest of the play. Discuss in your group which scenes will present problems and which may offer new insights.

Discuss also the new light shed on Claudius by such an interpretation; is there enough evidence in the text to justify such a view of him?

1989–1990 Royal Shakespeare Company's production of HAMLET in modern dress.

Shakespeare: an active approach **29**

11 • Group Dialogue

FOCUS ON: LANGUAGE

WHOLE CLASS ACTIVITY

KNOWLEDGE OF PLAY REQUIRED

Procedure

Get a couple of volunteers to read the dialogue through to the rest of the group. Then divide the class into two groups : one is to be Ophelia and one Hamlet.

Ask each member to choose a phrase or line from this scene (Act III.i.) which seems to encapsulate the attitude of their character. Then get them to deliver these lines in turn, one alternately from each of the two groups. (It doesn't matter at all if two or more students choose the same lines – the point is to get the 'feel' of the dialogue and the emotions underlying it.)

The next stage is to concentrate on Hamlet's 'Get thee to a nunnery' speech and Ophelia's responses. Choose one student to represent Ophelia and have him or her kneeling in the middle of a circle made up of all the rest of the class, who represent Hamlet. Divide Hamlet's lines between them according to the marks on the text and give them time to repeat them over and over until they have memorised them.

Now run through all lines in the right order so that they can learn their cues. From then on it is up to the group to suggest movements, effects, ways of delivering lines, that will bring out the conflict between Hamlet and Ophelia in a dramatic way, and the dialogue can be rehearsed a few times until they are satisfied with the 'performance'.

Other examples

The exchange between Laertes and Hamlet over Ophelia's grave works well (Act V.i. 235-76). Also Hamlet and Gertrude in the Closet scene (Act III.iv.88-109).

Follow-up

A context-type question on the passage could follow, in the hope that the understanding of language and mood will be enhanced by the dramatic exploration.

11 • Group Dialogue

FOCUS ON: LANGUAGE

Example

Ophelia My lord, I have remembrances of yours.
  That I have longed long to re-deliver.
  I pray you now receive them.
Hamlet   No, not I,
  I never gave you aught.
Ophelia My honoured lord, you know right well you
    did,
  And with them words of so sweet breath composed
  As made these things more rich. Their perfume lost,
  Take these again, for to the noble mind
  Rich gifts wax poor when givers prove unkind.
  There my lord.
Hamlet Ha, ha, are you honest?
Ophelia My lord?
Hamlet Are you fair?
Ophelia What means your lordship?
Hamlet That if you be honest and fair, your honesty
    should admit no discourse to your beauty.
Ophelia Could beauty, my lord, have better commerce
    than with honesty?
Hamlet Ay truly, for the power of beauty will sooner
    transform honesty from what is to a bawd, than
    the force of honesty can translate beauty into his
    likeness. This was sometime a paradox, but now the
    time gives it proof. I did love you once.
Ophelia Indeed my lord you made me believe so.
Hamlet You should not have believed me, for virtue
    cannot so inoculate our old stock, but we shall relish
    of it. I loved you not.
Ophelia I was the more deceived.
Hamlet Get thee to a nunnery, why wouldst thou be a
    breeder of sinners/I am myself indifferent honest but
    yet I could accuse me of such things,/ that it were
    better my mother had not borne me/I am very proud,
    revengeful, ambitious/with more offences at my beck/
    than I have thoughts to put them in/imagination to
    give them shape/or time to act them in/What should
    such fellows as I do/crawling between earth and
    heaven/We are arrant knaves all, believe none of us/

Go thy ways to a nunnery/Where's your father/
Ophelia At home my lord.
Hamlet Let the doors be shut upon him, that he may
    play the fool no where but in 's own house. Farewell.
Ophelia O help him, you sweet heavens!
Hamlet If thou dost marry, I'll give thee this plague for
    thy dowry—be thou as chaste as ice, as pure as snow,
    thou shalt not escape calumny. Get thee to a nunnery,
    go, farewell. Or if thou wilt needs marry, marry a fool
    for wise men know well enough what monsters you
    make of them. To a nunnery go, and quickly too.
    Farewell.

From Act III.i.

Activity

You are going to present parts of this dialogue as a group performance, taking individual phrases of either Hamlet or Ophelia and trying to bring out the meaning and mood of the exchanges between them.

First of all, re-read the passage to remind yourselves of what is said and why it is said. Try to think what has made Hamlet so aggressive towards the girl he seems to have once loved, and of how Ophelia is feeling, knowing as she does that her father and Claudius are listening nearby.

When you have been given a line, repeat it a number of times to yourself in different tones of voice, experimenting with the meaning and the implications you can get out of it. Try to learn your piece by heart before you put it together with the other lines to recreate the dialogue. Remember you are not trying to act as these two characters, but rather to capture the mood and effect of the scene.

Follow-up

Write some notes of your own about what you have added to your knowledge of Hamlet and Ophelia from the work on this dialogue.

12 • Missing Punctuation

FOCUS ON: VERSE/LANGUAGE

INDIVIDUAL WORK

KNOWLEDGE OF PLAY NOT REQUIRED

Procedure

Give the students a few minutes to read the chosen passage for themselves and to mark the 'sense units' with vertical pencil lines. Sit them in a circle and ask them to read, in turn round the circle, the next whole sense unit which they can identify. Go round again if necessary until the whole passage is used up.

Now continue round the circle, asking them this time to read one *line* each, the metrical unit this time – but still retaining the sense – for instance, by keeping the voice up at the end of the line if the sense continues into the next. Several attempts, with discussion in between, may be necessary before the version meets with general approval.

The next stage is to pick out certain *key words* – notable either for sense or for sound effect – which emerge from these readings. The tensions of the two patterns existing in counterpoint – the metre and the syntax – will become clearer than with a plain reading of the text; then a comparison with the editor's punctuation will also stimulate discussion of the minimal, but dramatic, punctuation in Quarto/Folio.

Examples

Two passages are offered, from HAMLET Act IV.v. and MACBETH Act IV.iii. but the idea is readily adaptable to any play, with the help of a little correction fluid and a photocopier.

Follow-up

This is a good way to introduce the idea of blank verse metre and to get the 'feel' of the characteristic rhythms of Shakespeare's verse, by active participation of students. It could also lead to a detailed commentary on the passage in terms of thought-development, imagery connections and the balance of sound and sense.

12 • *Missing Punctuation*

FOCUS ON: VERSE/LANGUAGE

Examples

Hamlet:

O this is the poison of deep grief it springs
All from her fathers death and now behold
O Gertrude Gertrude
When sorrows come they come not single spies
But in battalions first her father slain
Next your son gone and he most violent author
Of his own just remove the people muddied
Thick and unwholesome in their thoughts and
　　whispers
For good Polonius death and we have done but
　　greenly
In huggermugger to inter him poor Ophelia
Divided from herself and her fair judgement
Without the which we are pictures or mere beasts
Last and as much containing as all these
Her brother is in secret come from France
Feeds on his wonder keeps himself in clouds
And wants not buzzers to infect his ear
With pestilent speeches of his fathers death
Wherein necessity of matter beggared
Will nothing stick our person to arraign
In ear and ear o my dear Gertrude this
Like to a murdering piece in many places
Gives me superfluous death

Macbeth:

Macduff this noble passion
Child of integrity hath from my soul
Wiped the black scruples reconciled my thought
To thy good truth and honour devilish Macbeth
By many of these trains hath sought to win me
Into his power and modest wisdom plucks me
From over credulous haste but god above
Deal between thee and me for even now
I put myself to thy direction and
Unspeak my own detraction here abjure
The taints and blames I laid upon myself
For strangers to my nature I am yet
Unknown to woman never was forsworn
Scarcely have coveted what was mine own
At no time broke my faith would not betray
The devil to his fellow and delight
No less in truth than life my first false speaking
Was this upon myself what I am truly
Is thine and my poor country's to command
Whither indeed before thy here approach
Old Siward with ten thousand warlike men
Already at a point was setting forth
Now we'll together and the chance of goodness
Be like our warranted quarrel

Activity

First of all try to make sense of the passage you are using.
When you have read it right through and got some idea of
the sequence of ideas, mark with a vertical pencil stroke
the 'sense units' – each phrase you feel would probably
warrant a comma, semi-colon or full stop in a modern
edition.

When you are reading aloud, try to listen to these units
(yours may well not be the same as other people's) and at
the same time listen to the rhythm of the line. Between
these two patterns you will find the 'feel' of the language
with important words, changes of direction and pauses
highlighted.

Follow-up

Cut out your passage and stick it in the centre of a larger
piece of paper. Now use the space round it to make your
own commentary on any points of interest like images,
rhythm and development of thought.

　　　　　Shakespeare: an active approach　**33**

13 • *Two-handed Soliloquy*

FOCUS ON: CHARACTER

PAIR WORK

KNOWLEDGE OF PLAY NOT REQUIRED

Procedure

Examples are given in the students' notes from HAMLET and MACBETH but other plays offer equally good opportunities.

Choose passages from soliloquies which involve dilemmas of some sort, or uncertainty and indecision.

The students, in pairs, are asked to present the speech as a dialogue – perhaps as though two conflicting ideas are being argued out inside the mind, or as though both readers are developing the argument or contributing thoughts to the exploration of the idea.

They can also devise dramatic ways of presenting the soliloquy and bringing out its meaning: perhaps a game of chess?; or two figures sitting back to back?; or one sitting, with the other circling round?

Other examples

1 HAMLET:
Hamlet: Now might I do it pat . . . III.iii.73-96.

How all occasions do inform against me . . . IV.iv.32-66.

2 MACBETH:
Lady Macbeth: Glamis thou art, and Cawdor . . .
I.v.15-30.

Macbeth: To be thus is nothing, but to be safely thus . . . III.i.47-71.

Follow-up

Some versions can be presented and discussed, and written answers on the chosen soliloquy would follow naturally.

13 • *Two-handed Soliloquy*

FOCUS ON: CHARACTER

Example

Hamlet:

To be, or not to be, that is the question:
Whether 'tis nobler in the mind to suffer
The slings and arrow of outrageous fortune,
Or to take arms against a sea of troubles,
And by opposing end them? To die, to sleep—
No more; and by a sleep to say we end
The heart-ache, and the thousand natural shocks
That flesh is heir to; 'tis a consummation
Devoutly to be wished. To die, to sleep—
To sleep, perchance to dream, ay theres the rub,
For in that sleep of death what dreams may come
When we have shuffled off this mortal coil,
Must give us pause; there's the respect
That makes calamity of so long life.
For who would bear the whips and scorns of time,
Th' oppressor's wrong, the proud man's contumely,
the pangs of despised love, the law's delay,
The insolence of office, and the spurns
That patient merit of the unworthy takes
When he himself might his quietus make
With a bare bodkin?

Act III.i.

Macbeth:

If it were done, when 'tis done, then 'twere well
It were done quickly. If th' assassination
Could trammel up the consequence, and catch
With his surcease, success; that but this blow
Might be the be-all and the end-all—here,
But here, upon this bank and shoal of time,
We'd jump the life to come. But in these cases
We still have judgement here, that we but teach
Bloody instructions, which being taught return
To plague th' inventor. This even-handed justice
Commends th' ingredience of our poisoned chalice
To our own lips. He's here in double trust:
First, as I am his kinsman and his subject,
Strong both against the deed; then, as his host,
Who should against his murderer shut the door,
Not bear the knife myself. Besides, this Duncan
Hath borne his faculties so meek, hath been
So clear in his great office, that his virtues
Will plead like angels, trumpet-tongued against
The deep damnation of his taking-off.
And pity, like a naked new-born babe,
Striding the blast, or heaven's cherubin, horsed
Upon the sightless couriers of the air,
Shall blow the horrid deed in every eye,
That tears shall drown the wind. I have no spur
To prick the sides of my intent, but only
Vaulting ambition, which o'erleaps itself,
And falls on th' other—

Act I.vii.

Activity

Present one of these speeches in dialogue form. You might use the two voices to represent opposing view points, or develop the thought of the passage by each voice contributing an idea in turn; sometimes you might speak together. Some pieces will demand whispered exchanges, some vigorous assertions. Try to devise a way of presenting your dialogue dramatically, with movement or symbolic positioning.

Follow-up

Cut out the speech you have worked on and stick it in the middle of a larger piece of paper. Use the space around it to attach your comments and thoughts about it, and keep it for revision.

Shakespeare: an active approach **35**

14 • *Sources*

Procedure

There is very little value in taking A-Level students through the detailed textual history of a play, but it can be a good idea to look at Shakespeare's use of his sources for a particular play, in a few carefully chosen details. These are not valuable in themselves but in drawing attention to what Shakespeare chose to do with them and how he altered them. These facts will supply clues as to what he wanted to emphasise, and will lead to discussion of character and themes.

The Students' Notes contain some extracts from Holinshed, almost the sole source for MACBETH and a note of other changes Shakespeare made in this material.

The introduction or appendix to any good edition of the play will provide plenty of further information.

Other examples

ANTONY AND CLEOPATRA: Look at the way Shakespeare changes Cleopatra from Plutarch's character, by adding her perversity and contrariness. Also, Plutarch shows the Seleucus scene to be quite clearly a prepared trick by Cleopatra to deceive Caesar : Shakespeare's is by no means so unambiguous.

CORIOLANUS : Volumnia is very much Shakespeare's creation, built on very little in Plutarch; he makes one single uprising out of a series of usury and corn riots; the popular welcome Coriolanus receives when he returns to Rome at the beginning is not in Plutarch; Plutarch's hero is a much more vindictive and petty figure, and Shakespeare manipulates his material to make him more noble and heroic.

All these would be worth investigating further and discussing.

Follow-up

In the case of MACBETH, the comparisons could lead to essays on Banquo or on Lady Macbeth's Sleepwalking scene.

14 • *Sources*

FOCUS ON: DRAMATIC EFFECT

> ### *Duncan's inadequacy as King.*
> The beginning of Duncans reigne was verie quiet and peaceable, without anie notable trouble; but after it was perceiued how negligent he was in punishing offendors, manie misruled persons tooke occasion thereof to trouble the peace and quiet state of the common-wealth, by seditious commotions which first had their beginnings in this wise.

> ### *Basis of the Apparition Scene*
> And suerlie herevpon had he put Makduffe to death, but that a certaine witch, whom hee had in great trust, had told that he should neuer be slaine with man borne of anie woman, nor vanquished till the wood of Bernane came to the castell of Dunsinane. By this prophesie Makbeth put all feare out of his heart, supposing he might doo what he would, without anie feare to be punished for the same, for by the one prophesie he beleeued it was vnpossible for anie man to vanquish him, and by the other vnpossible to slea him. This vaine hope caused him to doo manie outragious things, to the greeuous oppression of his subjects.

> ### *Banquo's complicity*
> At length therefore, communicating his purposed intent with his trustie friends, amongst whome Banquho was the chiefest, vpon confidence of their promised aid, he slue the king at Enuerns, or (as some say) at Botgosuane, in the sixt yeare of his reigne.

> ### *Servants hired to murder King.*
> Then Donwald, though he abhorred the act greatlie in heart, yet through instigation of his wife hee called foure of his seruants vnto him (whome he had made priuie to his wicked intent before, and framed to his purpose with large gifts) and now declaring vnto them, after what sort they should worke the feat, they gladlie obeied his instructions, & speedilie going about the murther, they enter the chamber (in which the king laie) a little before cocks crow, where they secretlie cut his throte as he lay sleeping, without anie buskling at all: and immediatlie by a posterne gate they caried foorth the dead bodie into the fieldes . . .

> ### *Macbeth's ten years of good rule.*
> These and the like commendable lawes Makbeth caused to be put as then in vse, gouerning the realme for the space of ten yeares in equall iustice. But this was but a counterfet zeale of equitie shewed by him, partlie against his naturall inclination to purchase thereby the fauour of the people.

Source: Holinshed; *Chronicles of Scotland,* 1577

> **Other alterations include:**
> - Shakespeare invents the banquet scene and Banquo's Ghost.
> - He invents the sleepwalking scene.

Activity

Shakespeare's main source for MACBETH was an Elizabethan historian called **Holinshed**, whose work also provided him with the stories for several others of his plays.

He combined in the play two of Holinshed's historical figures: a man called Donwald, who, at the instigation of his wife, murdered King Duff, his guest at the time, putting the blame on the king's two drunken chamberlains, and, secondly, Makbeth, the murderer of King Duncan.

What is interesting about these sources is not so much what Shakespeare took from them but how much he altered them. This information will help us to see what he wanted to stress and underline in some of his characters and themes.

Make your own notes on the most obvious alterations you can spot in the extracts and examples given, and speculate on what might have been his reasons for them.

Follow-up

Three pieces of writing to explore these ideas a stage further:

1 What do you think is added to the audience's perception of Lady Macbeth by the addition of the Sleepwalking scene?

2 What view of Banquo is Shakespeare presenting? He shows us a man innocent of the complicity Holinshed reveals, but is he completely free of guilt? Look at III.i.1-10. and the conversation with Macbeth which follows.

3 Comment on the theatrical effectiveness of the Apparition scene (IV.i.).

15 • *Bare Bones: Speech*

FOCUS ON: LANGUAGE

PAIR WORK

KNOWLEDGE OF PLAY NOT REQUIRED

Procedure

Ask the students, in pairs, to look at the given speech (or prepare some alternatives and give the pairs a variety of pieces to do). Ask them to reduce this passage to its 'bare bones', selecting the most important phrases and connecting them with the fewest possible words of their own.

Give them a maximum, say, of ten lines, in which to encapsulate the essence of the speech, and then get them to perform the result to the rest of the class.

The discussion which follows is, of course, the most important element in the exercise. What has been lost? If they have removed most of the imagery, which is likely, how does this change our perceptions of the passage? Has it lost those qualities which gave it the distinctive voice of the character speaking? What would be the dramatic effect of the emasculated version?

This can be a useful way of focusing attention on the qualities of a particular speech; it is worth going back to the original for a final reading after the discussion.

Further examples

Lady Macbeth: The raven himself is hoarse . . .' I.v. 38–57. Macbeth; 'To be thus is nothing, but to be safely thus . . .' III.i.47–71.

Follow-up

This is a good preparation for the kind of A-Level question which asks of a context passage, 'How does the language used by Macbeth here convey his state of mind?' or 'Show how the imagery contributes to the effect of this passage'.

15 • Bare Bones: Speech

FOCUS ON: LANGUAGE

Example

Is this a dagger, which I see before me,
The handle toward my hand? Come, let me clutch
     thee:–
I have thee not, and yet I see thee still.
Art thou not, fatal vision, sensible
To feeling, as to sight? or art thou but
A dagger of the mind, a false creation,
Proceeding from the heat-oppressed brain?
I see thee yet, in form as palpable
As this which now I draw.
Thou marshall'st me the way that I was going;
And such an instrument I was to use.–
Mine eyes are made the fools o'th'other senses,
Or else worth all the rest: I see thee still;
And on thy blade, and dudgeon, gouts of blood,
Which was not so before.–There's no such thing.

It is the bloody business which informs
Thus to mine eyes.–Now o'er the one half-world
Nature seems dead, and wicked dreams abuse
The curtain'd sleep: Witchcraft celebrates
Pale Hecate's off' rings; and wither'd Murther,
Alarum'd by his sentinel, the wolf,
Whose howl's his watch, thus with his stealthy pace,
With Tarquin's ravishing strides, towards his design
Moves like a ghost.–Thou sure and firm-set earth,
Hear not my steps, which way they walk, for fear
They very stones prate of my where-about,
And take the present horror from the time,
Which now suits with it.–Whiles I threat, he lives:
Words to the heat of deeds too cold breath gives.
                                        [*A bell rings.*
I go, and it is done: the bell invites me.
Hear it not, Duncan; for it is a knell
That summons thee to Heaven, or to Hell.   [*Exit.*

Nicol Williamson as Macbeth.

Activity

Read the passage carefully and decide how you can reduce it to its 'bare bones'. Start by underlining all the key phrases; retain the statements which seem straight-forward and remove the metaphors as far as you can. Using the minimum of your own words to make connections and link vital sections, reduce it to about ten to twelve lines. Don't expect it to sound much like the original but do make sure it is understandable by a newcomer to the play. (It need not, of course, be in blank verse!)

You will now have a chance to compare versions with the rest of the class and to discuss what has been lost from the original speech in terms of imagery and character.

Follow-up

This is useful preparation for context work or other extract-based questions.

16 • *Running Commentary*

FOCUS ON: CHARACTER

WHOLE CLASS ACTIVITY

KNOWLEDGE OF PLAY REQUIRED

Procedure

Two volunteers (plus a Lady Macbeth for her one line) read this dialogue through to themselves. Then ask the class to think of the context in which the scene takes place: remind them that Banquo has been a witness to Macbeth's meeting with the witches, was also present when Duncan's body was discovered, and has probably put two and two together. Ask them to look also at his soliloquy at the very beginning of Act III.

Now arrange the two readers facing one another, with half the class sitting behind each of them. They are to be the *thoughts* of the character they back, and must utter whatever they think is going through that character's mind.

Banquo and Macbeth then read the dialogue — with pauses which freeze time between the speeches — and in these gaps the thoughts are spoken spontaneously by their 'minds'.

It will probably take a few dry runs before they get the idea and lose their inhibitions, but the result will stimulate a good deal of discussion about the motivation and suspicion of the two of them.

Other examples

Another scene which lends itself to this treatment is the dialogue between Macbeth and Lady Macbeth in Act.vii.28–82, where there are plenty of opportunities for secret thoughts.

The activity is of course adaptable to other plays.

Follow-up

Exercises like this provide useful preparation for essay work; for example Banquo is traditionally seen as the 'good guy', but it could be that it is not so much the fear of Macbeth's power which prevents his speaking out as his own prospects of fathering a line of kings.

The second suggested passage reveals a good deal about the relationship between Macbeth and his wife and could be contrasted with the plans for murdering Mady Macduff — 'Be innocent of the knowledge, dearest chuck. . .'

16 • Running Commentary

FOCUS ON: CHARACTER

Example

Macbeth   Here's our chief guest.
Lady Macbeth   If he had been forgotten
   It had been, as a gap in our great feast,
   And all-thing unbecoming.
Macbeth   Tonight we hold a solemn supper sir,
   And I'll request your presence.
Banquo   Let your Highness
   Command upon me, to the which my duties
   Are with a most indissoluble tie
   For ever knit.
Macbeth   Ride you this afternoon?
Banquo   Ay, my good lord.
Macbeth We should have else desired your good advice,
   Which still hath been both grave and prosperous,
   In this day's council; but we'll take tomorrow.
   Is't far you ride?
Banquo   As far, my lord, as will fill up the time
   'Twixt this and supper. Go not my horse the better,
   I must become a borrower of the night
   For a dark hour or twain.
Macbeth   We hear our bloody cousins are bestowed
   In England and in Ireland, not confessing
   Their cruel parricide, filling their hearers
   With strange invention. But of that tomorrow,
   When therewithal we shall have cause of state
   Craving as jointly. Hie you to horse. Adieu,
   Till you return at night. Goes Fleance with you?
Banquo   As my good lord; our time does call upon's.
Macbeth   I wish your horses swift, and sure of foot;
   And so I do commend you to their backs.
   Farewell.   [*Exit Banquo*
   Let every man be master of his time
   Till seven at night; to make society
   The sweeter welcome, we will keep ourself
   Till supper-time alone. While then, God be with you!

from Act III.i.

Activity

Remind yourself, by looking in your text, where this passage comes from and of what has happened so far. Concentrate on the thoughts running through the minds of the two main speakers. Take a few minutes to pencil in a few ideas of what they might be thinking at certain points in the dialogue. (Remember we are not concerned with things that might really be spoken aloud but with those thoughts that neither would dare to utter.)

Follow-up

Use this passage as a starting point for a consideration of Banquo's character. Why, when he must suspect Macbeth's guilt, does he keep silent? Look at his soliloquy at the very beginning of Act III and see what you can read into that. The conversation earlier, at the beginning of Act II, is also worth careful consideration.

Bernard Hill as Macbeth and Joseph Marcell as Banquo in the 1985 production of MACBETH at the Leicester Haymarket.

    Shakespeare: an active approach

17 • *Bystanders*

FOCUS ON: PLOT/DRAMATIC EFFECT
INDIVIDUAL WORK
KNOWLEDGE OF PLAY REQUIRED

Procedure

On the principle that 'onlookers see more of the game', it is a good idea to ask the class to focus on events at some dramatic moment in the play from the point of view of a bystander.

Shakespeare's stage directions often indicate the presence of courtiers, attendants, soldiers, and sometimes their presence is implied, if not stated, by the nature of a scene. The opening of KING LEAR, for instance, is a ceremonial full-dress occasion, and 'Attendants' accompany the entrance of Lear. Similarly, in Act I.ii. of HAMLET, Claudius's address to the Court is clearly a public pronouncement, not a family conference, and he enters with Councillors and 'others'. These silent observers would surely report on events afterwards, back home?

Students will enjoy thinking themselves into these characters and reporting what has been happening from their point of view. Some lively and imaginative accounts can result from this exercise.

Variation: There can also be an expansion of the roles of those in the play who are onlookers for much of the time, though not all. Horatio, in HAMLET, for instance, acts as confidant and observer much of the time, and the report he makes to Fortinbras after the end of the play would make interesting reading.

Example

The scene chosen is the Banquet scene from MACBETH, which affords perhaps the best opportunity for students to record their grasp of events and, at the same time, imagine the theatrical effect, as any 'extra' in the scene would have to do.

Follow-up

Scripted scenes of the dialogue back home, or improvisations, would allow 'performance' to share the ideas.

17 • *Bystanders*

FOCUS ON: PLOT/DRAMATIC EFFECT

Example

Macbeth   Here had we now our country's honour roof'd,
  Were the grac'd person of our Banquo present;

The Ghost of BANQUO *enters, and sits* in MACBETH's *place*

  Who may I rather challenge for unkindness,
  Than pity for mischance!
Ross   His absence, Sir,
  Lays blame upon his promise. Please't your Highness
  To grace us with your royal company?
Macbeth   The table's full.
Lennox   Here is a place reserv'd, Sir.
Macbeth   Where?
Lennox   Here, my good Lord. What is't that moves your Highness?
Macbeth   Which of you have done this?
Lords   What, my good Lord?
Macbeth   Thou cans't not say, I did it: never shake Thy gory locks at me.
Ross   Gentlemen, rise; his Highness is not well.
Lady Macbeth   Sit, worthy friends. My Lord is often thus,
    And hath been from his youth: pray you, keep seat;
    The fit is momentary; upon a thought
    He will again be well. If much you note him,
    You shall offend him, and extend his passion;
    Feed and regard him not.—Are you a man?
Macbeth   Ay, and a bold one, that dare look on that Which might appal the Devil.
Lady Macbeth   O proper stuff!
    This is the very painting of your fear:
    This is the air-drawn dagger, which, you said,
    Led you to Duncan. O! these flaws and starts
    (Imposters to true fear), would well become
    A woman's story at a winter's fire,
    Authoris'd by her grandam. Shame itself!
    Why do you make such faces? When all's done,
    You look but on a stool.
Macbeth   Pr'ythee, see there!
    Behold! look! lo! how say you?
    Why, what care I? If thou cans't not, speak too.—
    If charnel-houses and our graves must send
    Those that we bury, back, our monuments
    Shall be the maws of kites.   *[Ghost disappears.*

Activity

Read the rest of this scene (Act III.iv.) in a copy of the play. Imagine that you are one of these lords or attendants mentioned in the stage directions and look through the scene again, thinking about what you would notice about Macbeth's behaviour. How would you react to Lady Macbeth's attempts to explain it away and calm the situation? How would you feel as you were invited to leave so unceremoniously?

Now write a **diary entry,** or a **letter to your family,** or an **interior monologue,** to express your thoughts and feelings. You can try to capture the flavour of the language and the period if you wish, or write in contemporary language, up-dating the situation.

Follow-up

1 Choose another time when a bystander could report on events – perhaps a soldier in Malcolm's army at the end, or a servant in Macbeth's castle when Duncan's body is discovered, and write your reactions.

2 Script a scene when such a person reports his account back at home afterwards.

Pip Miller as Macbeth and Nina Holloway as Lady Macbeth in the 1986 production of MACBETH at the Northcott Theatre.

18 • Opening as Novel

FOCUS ON: DRAMATIC FORM
INDIVIDUAL WORK
KNOWLEDGE OF PLAY REQUIRED

Procedure

The purpose of this exercise is to focus on the vital differences between plays and novels. Too many students still write in their essays, 'In the book. . . ', and seem less aware than they should be of the nature of a play, a form which is only fully realised in the interaction of actor, playwright and audience in performance.

One way to raise their awareness is to ask them to write the opening paragraphs of the novel *Macbeth*.

Discuss with them first some of the choices of structure and style open to them; a few are suggested in the Students' Notes.

Examples

This activity can apply equally well to any play with an 'atmospheric' opening: HAMLET works well as the opening seems like a good ghost story.

KING LEAR lends itself better to a retrospective structure – perhaps Edgar at the end thinking back over the events of the play and remembering how it all started. This adds a new discipline to the storyline as they will have to decide how much he knew about what was going on.

In THE TEMPEST the storm in novel form can provide a good contrast to the highly theatrical effects of the opening scene.

In all these cases, the comparison will bring out the nature of the dramatic form.

Follow-up

Find a way of sharing the writing that results from this; pass them round or display on the wall.

A-Level questions often ask about the 'dramatic effectiveness' of a scene or dialogue, i.e. how it would impress an audience in the theatre. This 'novel writing' will offer a starting point for such an essay.

18 • Opening as Novel

FOCUS ON: DRAMATIC FORM

Example

SCENE I   *[An open space.]*

Thunder and lightning. Enter three WITCHES

1 Witch When shall we three meet again?
   In thunder, lightning, or in rain?
2 Witch When the hurlyburly's done,
   When the battle's lost and won.
3 Witch That will be ere the set of sun.
1 Witch Where the place?
2 Witch   Upon the heath.
3 Witch There to meet with Macbeth.
1 Witch I come, Graymalkin!
2 Witch Paddock calls.
3 Witch Anon!
All Fair is foul, and foul is fair:
   Hover through the fog and filthy air.　　　*[Exeunt.*

Activity

Perhaps you have seen a production of MACBETH and have felt the sense of mystery and evil created by these few lines but, even if you haven't, you can hear the effect of the rhyme and incantatory rhythms, and imagine the atmosphere that could be created in the theatre.

If MACBETH were a novel – say, by Dickens – how could the same effect be achieved? Try writing the opening paragraphs of such a novel, taking care not to overdo the horror in case you make it unintentionally funny. Think about the choices open to the writer of the novel, *Macbeth*. He or she is not bound by the same restrictions of time and space as the dramatist; he or she can comment and intervene to draw the reader's attention to any particular thoughts and feelings of the characters. The whole story can be told through the eyes of one of the characters, perhaps by adopting a stream-of-consciousness approach. The story doesn't have to start at the beginning, it could be largely 'flashback'. It could be told in diary or letter form.

Consider all these possibilities and develop your opening chapter.

Follow-up

Discuss what the essential differences are between novels and plays. What is it that makes the opening of the play MACBETH so effective? Make notes on these points to keep for revision.

19 • *Letters*

FOCUS ON: PLOT

INDIVIDUAL WORK

KNOWLEDGE OF PLAY REQUIRED

Procedure

The students are asked to look up the references given and to make their own brief notes. It would be helpful for them to go over what they have found out and to discuss the importance of the letters in general.

Before they write their own versions of some of the letters referred to in the text, remind them to think about choosing a suitable style and tone.

Examples

Most important seem to be:

- Edmund's forged letter from his brother which forms the basis of his deception of Gloucester (1 on students' sheet).
- The letter Gloucester has received about the invasion by France and Cordelia, about which he confides in Edmund and thus seals his own fate. (4)

- The letter for Edmund discovered by Edgar when he kills Goneril's messenger, Oswald, (8), and which eventually brings about Edmund's downfall. There is an irony about this and a certain justice, that Edmund's plots began with a letter and it is a letter which reveals both his and Goneril's guilt (11).

Other plays

There are none where letters play such an important part in the plot but there are plenty of occasions when a letter could be imagined, in order to bring out a character's thoughts and feelings.

Follow-up

Letters written by the students could be circulated, or displayed, and then discussed. Any written work on the development of the plot could benefit from this preparatory analysis.

19 • Letters

FOCUS ON: PLOT

Example

Letters play a very important part in the plot of KING LEAR; events at many points turn on them and on their interception. Look up the following passages;

1 Act I.ii.24-5, 45-52
2 I.iv.334; I.v.1-6 (received by Regan: II.i.121-3)
3 Act III.i.30
4 III.iii.10-15 and 21-5 (see also III.vii.1-3 and 47-49)
5 Act IV.ii.82
6 IV.iii.10-32
7 IV.v.19-22
8 IV.vi.245-275
9 Act V.i.40-50
10 V.iii.26-7
11 V.iii.158

Activity

Make your own [...] these letters: what they cont[...] are [...]ed, and any importance they [...] in the plot. (For some of them we are given the actual text of the letter; others we have to deduce from the [...] evidence given...)

Choose two of the latter and write your own version of the letters. Try to capture the style of the writer as well as including the vital information, and reveal the relationship of sender and receiver by the tone you choose.

Follow-up

Try to think of some other occasions when a letter from one of the characters to another might well have been written, and invent one of your own, to reflect that person's reactions to events and situations.

20 • Role Play: Case Conference

FOCUS ON: LEAR

GROUP WORK

KNOWLEDGE OF PLAY REQUIRED

Procedure

This is another activity which forces students to look closely at the play to find evidence.

Divide the class into groups of four or five and get them to allocate roles, within the group, of:

>Cordelia
>Doctor
>Kent
>Psychiatrist
>Any other relevant character.

The Case Conference which ensues should address itself to these questions:

- What has caused Lear's madness?
- What are his symptoms?
- What treatment should be prescribed?

Evidence should be drawn primarily from the play itself, but clearly students will want to improvise as well, and air their own theories about Lear's situation and how far he himself has brought it about. The Fool would also provide an interesting witness.

Other examples of role play situations

From HAMLET: **A Press Conference** given by Claudius, soon after taking over as King, supported by Polonius. Reporters ask him about his accession and the death of old Hamlet.
Trial of Polonius for causing death of Ophelia.

From CORIOLANUS: **War Cabinet meeting.**
Coriolanus with his Psychiatrist.

Follow-up

Reports or newspaper accounts of these events offer a way of re-inforcing points which emerge.

20 · Role Play: Case Conference

FOCUS ON: LEAR

Example

Cordelia Alack! 'tis he: why, he was met even now
   As mad as the vex'd sea; singing aloud;
   Crown'd with rank fumiter and furrow-weeds,
   With hardocks, hemlock, nettles, cuckoo-flowers,
   Darnel, and all the idle weeds that grow
   In our sustaining corn. A century send forth;
   Search every acre in the high-grown field,
   And bring him to our eye.   *[Exit an Officer.*
                     What can man's wisdom
   In the restoring his bereaved sense?
   He that helps him take all my outward worth.
Doctor There is means, Madam;
   Our foster-nurse of nature is repose.
   The which he lacks; that to provoke in him,
   Are many simples operative, whose power
   Will close the eye of anguish.
Cordelia   All bless'd secrets,
   All you unpublish'd virtues of the earth,
   Spring with my tears! be aidant and remediate
   In the good man's distress! Seek, seek for him,
   Lest his ungovern'd rage dissolve the life
   That wants the means to lead it.

Activity

Set up a Case Conference about Lear between a psychiatrist and the interested parties but without Lear himself.

Think about the first symptoms of Lear's madness, the stages of insanity he goes through in the play and how he is found by Cordelia's attendants and brought to her.

Imagine that it is at this point that you are looking at his case; try to reach some conclusions about what has caused his loss of wits, his symptoms and any proposed treatment.

Follow-up

Write the psychiatrist's report on this conference, making sure you refer to evidence from the play itself and not just theories about it.

21 • *Happy Ending?*

FOCUS ON: TRAGEDY

CLASS DISCUSSION

KNOWLEDGE OF PLAY REQUIRED

Procedure

Nahum Tate's version of KING LEAR, despite several centuries of popularity during which it and variations on it virtually took over from Shakespeare's play on the London stage, is a curiosity rather than a real contribution to thinking about the play, but it can be useful in bringing out the special qualities of Shakespearian tragedy and especially the sense of pain and yet reconciliation which so often marks the end of a tragic play.

The ending of KING LEAR is perhaps the most painful of all, and least satisfies our sense of justice, yet we find Tate's version laughable and far *less* satisfying.

Discussion should centre on:

- the absence of the Fool from the play altogether;

- the motive for Cordelia's refusal to join her sisters in flattery of Lear;

- the exaggeration of the evil of the villains;

- the romantic 'happy ending'.

All these points should send students back to the original to find out exactly how Shakespeare did it and to look for textual evidence to support their views.

N.B. There are **two** students' sheets to go with this activity.

Examples

1 What does the play lose by the omission of the Fool theatrically and emotionally? What part does the Fool play in bringing Lear to a realisation of his own faults?

2 How does Tate's play modify our view of Cordelia? What are the motives Shakespeare gives for her refusal to flatter Lear?

3 Why should Tate feel the need to include Edmund's attempted rape of Cordelia? Why does he give Goneril the role of ordering the deaths of Lear and Cordelia?

4 Nahum Tate's play is consistent: it is a romantic play with melodrama, and all the action leads to the moral that 'Truth and Vertue shall at last succeed', but KING LEAR is a very different play. Contrast the way both plays end.

Follow-up

From the discussion, essay work on the Fool and on Cordelia can evolve. It could be a good point at which to introduce some of Aristotle's ideas about Tragedy, and to discuss the peculiar combination of justice and pain inherent in Shakespeare's greatest tragedies. (See Unit on Tragic Hero: CORIOLANUS).

21ᴀ • *Happy Ending?*

FOCUS ON: TRAGEDY

Example

In the first part of this last scene, Lear succeeds in striking down two of those who come to kill him and Cordelia in prison, and is himself rescued from others by the timely arrival of Edgar and Albany.

Bring in old *Kent,* and, *Edgar,* guide you hither
Your Father, whom you said was near, [*Exit* Edgar.
He may be an Ear-witness at the least
Of our Proceedings.
     Kent *brought in here.*
Lear Who are you?
My Eyes are none o'th'best, I'll tell you streight;
Oh *Albany!* Well, Sir, we are your Captives,
And you are come to see Death pass upon us.
Why this Delay? — or is't your Highness pleasure
To give us first the Torture? Say ye so?
Why here's old *Kent* and I, as tough a Pair
As e'er bore Tyrant's Stroke: — but my *Cordelia,*
My poor *Cordelia* here, O pitty! —
Albany Take off their Chains — Thou injur'd Majesty,
The Wheel of Fortune now has made her Circle,
And Blessings yet stand 'twixt thy Grave and Thee.
Lear Com'st Thou, inhumane Lord, to sooth us back
To a Fool's Paradise of Hope, to make
Our Doom more wretched? Go too, we are too well
Acquainted with Misfortune to be gull'd
With Lying Hope; No, we will hope no more.
Albany I have a Tale t' unfold so full of Wonder
As cannot meet an easy Faith;
But by that Royal injur'd Head 'tis True.
Kent What wou'd your Highness?
Albany   Know the noble *Edgar*
Impeacht Lord *Edmund* since the Fight, of Treason,
And dar'd him for the Proof to single Combat,
In which the Gods confirm'd his Charge by Conquest;
I left ev'n now the Traytor wounded Mortally.
Lear And whither tends this Story?
Albany   E'er they fought
Lord *Edgar* gave into my Hands this Paper,
A blacker Scrowl of Treason, and of Lust
Than can be found in the Records of Hell;
There, Sacred Sir, behold the Character
Of *Gonerill* the worst of Daughters, but
More Vicious Wife.
Cordelia Could there be yet Addition to their Guilt?
What will not They that wrong a Father doe?

Albany Since then my Injuries, *Lear,* fall in with Thine:
I have resolv'd the same Redress for Both.
Kent What says my Lord?
Cordelia   Speak, for methought I heard
The charming Voice of a descending God.
Albany The Troops by *Edmund* rais'd, I have disbanded;
Those that remain are under my Command.
What Comfort may be brought to cheer your Age
And heal your savage Wrongs, shall be apply'd;
For to your Majesty we do Resign
Your Kingdom, save what Part your Self conferr'd
On Us in marriage.
Kent   Hear you that, my Liege?
Cordelia Then there are Gods, and Vertue is their Care.
Lear Is't Possible?
Let the Spheres stop their Course, the Sun make Hault,
The Winds be husht, the Seas and Fountains Rest;
All Nature pause, and listen to the Change.
Where is my *Kent,* my *Cajus?*
Kent   Here, my Liege.
Lear Why I have News that will recall thy youth;
Ha! Didst Thou hear't, or did th'inspiring Gods
Whisper to me Alone? Old *Lear* shall be
A King again.
Kent The Prince, that like a God has Pow'r, has said it.
Lear Cordelia then shall be a Queen, mark that:
Cordelia shall be Queen; Winds catch the Sound
And bear it on your rosie Wings to Heav'n.
Cordelia is a Queen.
     Re-enter Edgar *with* Gloster.
Albany Look, Sir, where pious Edgar comes
Leading his Eye-less Father: O my Liege!
His wondrous Story will deserve your Leisure:
What He has done and suffer'd for your Sake,
What for the Fair *Cordelia's.*
Gloster Where is my Liege? Conduct me to his Knees to hail
His second Birth of Empire; my dear *Edgar*
Has, with himself, reveal'd the King's blest Restauration.
Lear My poor dark *Gloster*
Gloster O let me kiss that once more sceptred Hand!
Lear Hold, Thou mistak'st the Majesty, Kneel here;
Cordelia has our Pow'r, *Cordelia's* Queen.
Speak, is not that the noble Suffring *Edgar.?*
Gloster My pious Son, more dear than my lost Eyes.
Lear I wrong'd Him too, but here's the fair Amends.

      Shakespeare: an active approach   **51**

21ʙ • *Happy Ending?*

Edgar Your leave, my Liege, for an unwelcome Message.
　Edmund (but that's a Trifle) is expir'd;
　What more will touch you, your imperious Daughters
　Gonerill and haughty *Regan*, both are Dead,
　Each by the other poison'd at a Banquet;
　This, Dying, they confest.
Cordelia O fatal Period of ill-govern'd Life!
Lear Ingratefull as they were, my Heart feels yet
　A Pang of Nature for their wretched Fall;—
　But, *Edgar*, I defer thy Joys too long:
　Thou serv'dst distrest *Cordelia;* take her Crown'd:
　Th'imperial Grace fresh Blooming on her Brow;
　Nay, *Gloster*, Thou hast here a Father's Right;
　Thy helping Hand t'heap Blessings on their Heads.
Kent Old *Kent* throws in his hearty Wishes too.
Edgar The Gods and You too largely recompence
　What I have done; the Gift strikes Merit Dumb.
Cordelia Nor do I blush to own my Self o'er-paid
　For all my Suffrings past.
Gloster Now, gentle Gods, give *Gloster* his Discharge.
Lear No, *Gloster*, Thou hast Business yet for Life;
　Thou, *Kent* and I, retir'd to some cool Cell
　Will gently pass our short reserves of Time
　In calm Reflections on our Fortunes past,
　Cheer'd with relation of the prosperous Reign
　Of this celestial Pair; Thus our Remains
　Shall in an even Course of Thought be past,
　Enjoy the present Hour, nor fear the Last.
Edgar Our drooping Country now erects her Head,
　Peace spreads her balmy Wings, and Plenty Blooms.
　Divine *Cordelia,* all the Gods can witness
　How much thy Love to Empire I prefer!
　Thy bright Example shall convince the World.
　(Whatever Storms of Fortune are decreed)
　That Truth and Vertue shall at last succeed.
　　　　　　　　　　　　[Exeunt Omnes.

Activity

Read this scene carefully. It is from a adaptation of KING LEAR written in 1681 by Nahum Tate. It was popular for a very long time and spawned a whole series of other happy-ending versions. Even the famous actor Garrick, whose greatest role was supposed to be King Lear, performed his own version of this in the mid-eighteenth century, rather than the Shakespeare play.

Besides this very different last scene, other significant alterations Tate made include:

- The Fool completely omitted;
- Cordelia 'lying' to her father in the first scene in order to avoid being married to Burgundy;
- Edgar's confession of love for Cordelia and her testing of him by pretended indifference;
- Increased villainy of Edmund (who tries at one point to rape Cordelia) and the wicked sisters. (It is Goneril who orders the execution of Lear and Cordelia.)

Follow-up

What does the play lose by the absence of the Fool? How does the ending in Tate's version alter the audience's feelings?

22 • On and Off

FOCUS ON: PLOT
INDIVIDUAL OR PAIR WORK
KNOWLEDGE OF PLAY REQUIRED

Procedure

In a fairly complex plot, and especially in a play where a sub-plot exists side by side with the main plot, students can find events confusing. This activity is designed to help them sort things out in their minds after a first reading of the play.

The chart is self-explanatory, but allows for the addition of extra codes to indicate important events, deaths, settings, etc which can be agreed in discussion with them. (To make the full chart, each student will need copies of pages 54 and 55 which should be overlapped and taped together on the back.)

Other examples

It is certainly worth using this idea with other plays as well.

In THE TEMPEST, for instance, it could make apparent the distribution of the Caliban-Trinculo-Stephano scenes between the main plot scenes.

ANTONY AND CLEOPATRA is so complicated that such analysis may prove almost impossible, but the attempt could be useful and could bring out shifts of setting from Rome to Egypt, and could even help to clarify the political plot and underline the confusing sequence of battles in Act IV. Perhaps in this case each student should only undertake a section of the play and share the information with the rest in some way.

Follow-up

Other visual ways of presenting storyline and plot can be explored (see also unit on **Thinking Visually**, pages 20–21). Some plays lend themselves to a kind of 'Snakes and Ladders' treatment, while others are better in a kind of Family Tree shape, with each act on a separate line, leading down to the next.

Shakespeare: an active approach

22 • On and Off

FOCUS ON: PLOT

Key

Example

	Lear	Cornwall	Albany	Kent	Gloucester	Edgar	Edmund	Oswald	Fool
I.i.									
I.ii.									
I.iii.									
I.iv.									
I.v.									
II.i.									
II.ii.									
II.iii.									
II.iv.									
III.i.									
III.ii.									
III.iii.									
III.iv.									
III.v.									
III.vi.									
III.vii.									
IV.i.									
IV.ii.									
IV.iii.									
IV.iv.									
IV.v.									
IV.vi.									
IV.vii.									
V.i.									
V.ii.									
V.iii.									

Activity

This exercise will help you to keep track of who is where, when, and why. Plot on the diagram the scenes which the characters appear in and mark in some way where the scene takes place, together with any important events you wish to include. (You might wish to distinguish the Gloucester sub-plot by using a different colour, or to find other ways of presenting information on your chart.)

Follow-up

The analysis will bring out some points very clearly, many of which are worth further exploration. For instance, why does the Fool disappear completely, with no real evidence of what has happened to him?

Goneril	Regan	Cordelia	Minor characters					Settings	Deaths etc

23 • Dumb Show

FOCUS ON: PLOT/REVISION
GROUP WORK
KNOWLEDGE OF PLAY REQUIRED

Procedure

It is a good idea to prepare students for the idea of using movement in a symbolic, stylised way by asking them to work in pairs and to mould each other into 'sculptures' symbolising abstract concepts like 'Greed', 'Hunger' or 'Pity'. Statues are then frozen and sculptors walk around to look at others' efforts. (See also **Freeze Frames** – another way into this activity.)

Now divide them into five groups and give them one act of the play each to work on. Their task is to present the important action, themes and characters of that act in mime and movement – without any words.

Encourage them to use slow-motion, in which each gesture means something and presents a clear-cut image; they shouldn't try to play out the whole act in detail, but to be selective.

If you have too small a group to make this exercise practical, confine it to one act and do it as a whole class.

Example

Act III would need to convey:

- the situation explained by Kent to gentleman;
- the storm and Lear's state of mind;
- Gloucester's confidence to Edmund about the letter;
- meeting with Poor Tom and Gloucester's help to Lear;
- Edmund's betrayal of his father;
- Lear's trial of Goneril and Regan in the farmhouse;
- Gloucester's eyes, and Cornwall's fatal wound.

Other plays

This method can be used with any other play but is especially valuable for complex action – like the last act of HAMLET or the constant switching of scene from Egypt to Rome, Syria and Actium, in Act III of ANTONY AND CLEOPATRA.

Follow-up

Discussion of what was made clear in each act and what was missed out can be useful for revision.

23 • Dumb Show

FOCUS ON: PLOT/REVISION

Example

Trumpets sound. The Dumb Show enters

Enter a KING and a QUEEN very lovingly; the QUEEN embracing him, and he her. She kneels, and makes show of protestation unto him. He takes her up, and declines his head upon her neck: lays him down upon a bank of flowers: she, seeing him asleep, leaves him. Anon comes in a fellow, takes off his crown, kisses it, and pours poison in the KING's ears, and exit. The QUEEN returns; finds the KING dead, and makes passionate action. The POISONER, with some two or three MUTES, comes in again, seeming to lament with her. The dead body is carried away. The POISONER wooes the QUEEN with gifts: she seems harsh awhile, but in the end accepts his love. *[Exeunt*

There are sequences of action in some of Shakespeare's plays which are presented to the audience in *Dumb Show*. One notable example is in HAMLET, where Hamlet arranges to have a play performed which will show the king, his uncle, that he is aware of how old Hamlet died. This play is preceded by the Dumb Show above, which mimes the play's main events.

You can see from the way the actions are described that they are stylised rather than realistic and that attention is drawn to certain symbolic actions, like the 'protestations' of the queen, the 'passionate' action of her grief, and the wooing with gifts.

Activity

Your task is to present a Dumb Show: the essence of your act in mime. You will need to convey what happens, of course, but also indicate the relationships of the characters and draw attention to themes and images which seem important to that act.

You may need to reduce the number of characters if there aren't enough of you, or to play several parts.

Remember to go for symbolism rather than realism and keep the gestures *big*. You are not acting out a summarised version of the play but focusing on what you see as the essentials.

Follow-up

Discuss other groups' versions of their acts and compare interpretations of characters who appear in more than one act.

Shakespeare: an active approach

24 • Role Play: Inquest

FOCUS ON: OVERVIEW OF PLAY/REVISION
WHOLE CLASS ACTIVITY/GROUP PREPARATION
KNOWLEDGE OF PLAY REQUIRED

Procedure

The class must be familiar with the whole play and preferably will have seen it performed. The exercise makes a good summing-up before moving on to a new text.

In discussion with the students, draw up a list of those who might conceivably be accused of contributing to the death and suffering of Lear. Keep this fairly short if you can – perhaps, Goneril and Regan; Edmund; Lear himself; Cordelia? (for her stubbornness at the beginning); Albany? (for his weak incompetence); Gloucester? (for his stupidity in being unable to distinguish between his sons).

Write the four or five chosen on cards and divide the class into the same number of groups as these, leaving two or three students to be the Coroners.

Each group then draws a card and is given the task of preparing evidence against their candidate, to present before the Coroners, who can meanwhile arrange the Courtroom, decide on running order and draw up a list of questions to ask the chief witnesses.

It is a good idea for you to be in role as well – if you are Clerk to the Court you can control the strict time limit which must be imposed on each group if all are to have a fair hearing.

Preparation will take a couple of lessons, and the performance whatever is allowed, plus some changeover time and time to consider the verdict.

Other examples

Other plays with which this works well are : MACBETH, and CORIOLANUS, for A-Level and *Romeo and Juliet* at GCSE Level.

In HAMLET, the Coroner's Court could sit on Ophelia's death.

Follow-up

The whole class could act as Jury and write their conclusions down for the Coroners, before the Coroners offer a reasoned judgement.

24 • Role Play: Inquest

FOCUS ON: OVERVIEW OF PLAY/REVISION

Example

Who is guilty of Lear's death and suffering? When did such a painful ending to the play become inevitable? At what point, and by whose actions and words, did the sequence of events begin?

No one character or one action, of course, can be held responsible, but many contributed to it. Think back over the whole play and pick out who was most guilty.

Activity

When you have drawn lots for characters, your group must search the play for evidence which points to your character's implication in the tragic outcome. The case may be presented in any way you like; you are not bound by courtroom procedures in this 'supernatural' inquest and can call equally on the living and the dead to testify. One way might be to have a Prosecuting Counsel, who calls witnesses to be questioned by him or her and by the Coroners, and who must answer in role to the best of their knowledge. Or you could have a Counsel who calls up in flashback scenes from the play to prove the case. Or perhaps freeze frames from the play to reconstruct vital scenes; or a combination of all these methods.

Follow-up

This activity can help with your revision of a play as it brings back vividly the main events and characters and at the same time makes you look again at important scenes and speeches.

25 • Openings

FOCUS ON: DRAMATIC SITUATION

INDIVIDUAL WORK

KNOWLEDGE OF ACT 1 REQUIRED

Procedure

Students will need to have read at least the first act to gain much from discussion of this opening passage.

When they have, they can visualise the scene and reconstruct the preceding conversation. This will provide them with insight into the contrasting worlds of Rome and Egypt. At the same time, it can make them aware of those features of production which lift the play off the page and make it more than a text for study.

Examples

Draw students' attention to the following contrasts between the worlds of Rome and Egypt:

1 Association of Egypt with games and entertainments: billiards, fishing, fortune telling, jokes (often risqué) and laughter.

2 Association of Rome with duty: Antony's need to return to Rome because of Fulvia's death ('I must from this enchanting queen break off.'); Octavia's sense of duty towards her brother, and Antony later, (Act III.ii., III.iv.) Caesar's disapproval of Antony's riotous behaviour (opening of Act I.iv.); Caesar's reluctance to indulge in the drunken celebrations on Pompey's barge (II.vii.97.); Cleopatra's 'Roman death' (V.ii.)

Other plays

KING LEAR: Kent and Gloucester are clearly in the middle of a conversation in the opening lines and to speculate about what might have preceded these words could introduce the relationship between Edmund, Edgar and Gloucester.

HAMLET: the urgency of Francisco's and Bernardo's challenges arises from the events of the past two nights: they both know the ghost has appeared twice and are expecting a third visit – enough to make anyone jumpy. An effective silent opening sequence could precede the lines.

Follow-up

Displays of set designs and/or 'performance' of preceding dialogues and sound effects will provoke discussion.

On ANTONY AND CLEOPATRA specifically, the activity can lead to written work on Antony's divided loyalties or to the contrasts between Rome and Egypt.

25 • Openings

FOCUS ON: DRAMATIC SITUATION

Example

Enter Demetrius and Philo

Philo   Nay, but this dotage of our general's
O'erflows the measure: those his goodly eyes
That o'er the files and musters of the war
Have glow'd like plated Mars, now bend, now turn,
The office and devotion of their view
Upon a tawny front: his captain's heart,
Which in the scuffles of great fights hath burst
The buckles on his breast, reneges all temper,
And is become the bellows and the fan
To cool a gipsy's lust. Look where they come:
Take but good note, and you shall see in him
The triple pillar of the world transformed
Into a strumpet's fool: behold and see.

Activity

It is immediately obvious that these lines are in mid-conversation. Why else should he start with 'Nay, but. . .'?

Imagine you are a director of a production of the play and that you have decided to open with some stage business rather than go straight into the opening words. What could you show on stage which might add extra point to Philo's words and perhaps illustrate the decadence of the Egyptian court as he sees it?

Describe in your own words the scene before you, specifying sound and lighting effects as well as action. If you prefer, treat it as film script and describe the opening shots which lead up to Philo's speech.

Now turn your attention to the conversation itself, and try to reconstruct what might have been said by Demetrius before these lines. Write your version of the preceding conversation, for you and a partner to present to the rest.

Follow-up

Design your set for this opening scene, which creates the impression of opulence and self-indulgence in Egypt, contrasting so strongly with Antony's Roman past. Where would you place Philo and Demetrius on the stage?

From your further reading of the play, make a list of contrasts between the worlds of Rome and Egypt.

Michael Redgrave as Antony and Peggy Ashcroft as Cleopatra in the 1953 production at the Shakespeare Memorial Theatre.

Shakespeare: an active approach

26 • Patterns of Imagery

FOCUS ON: LANGUAGE

INDIVIDUAL OR GROUP WORK

KNOWLEDGE OF PLAY REQUIRED

Procedure

Students need to look up the contexts of the quotations given and to see them in relation to the surrounding language.

Discussion should then centre on the light they shed on themes and characters in the play; students may need to be reminded that each time we notice an image recurring, it comes to us with the added force of the previous occurrences and that the effect is cumulative.

The 'games and pastimes' images recur so often that they come to symbolise the essential quality of Egypt, as opposed to the duty and military discipline of Rome.

There are of course many such groups of images in the play and those listed here are only a beginning in the work of identifying and linking them.

Other examples

Each play has its own patterns of imagery, some more obvious than others, and all are worth exploring with students.

HAMLET: Images of death and decay, and of things appearing to be what they are not, abound, but there is also a pattern of parallels between people and beasts, which implies that people have a choice – to be like the angels or like the beasts.

MACBETH: Imagery of blood, night and darkness are immediately apparent, but there is also the idea of clothes, particularly ill-fitting ones, to represent honours and rank.

KING LEAR: Images of sight and blindness are pretty evident, but there is also a recurring theme of birds of prey and wild beasts, especially applied to Goneril and Regan.

THE TEMPEST: Music and dance (reaching its height in the Masque) symbolise order and control, reinforced by images of plenty and fulfilment. The sea, particularly its power to change and renew, is a more obvious motif.

Follow-up

Divide students into five groups and give each group an act of the play; ask them to list the images they find, under previously agreed headings.

The resulting information should be displayed or photocopied for all.

26 • *Patterns of Imagery*

FOCUS ON: LANGUAGE

Examples

There are a number of threads of imagery which run through the play, and which we notice gradually, as they recur. Look at these two sets of quotations:

A   Images of riches and of extravagance of eating and drinking

1 Say the firm Roman to great Egypt sends this treasure of an oyster.   **I.v.43-44.**

2 I'll set thee in a shower of gold and hail
   Rich pearls upon thee.   **II.v.44-45.**

3 I' the market-place, on a tribunal silver'd,
   Cleopatra and himself in chairs of gold
   Were publicly enthroned.   **III.v.3-6.**

4 I'll give thee friend,
   An armour all of gold.   **IV.viii.26-27.**

5 . . .the poop was beaten gold;
   Purple the sails and so perfumed that
   The winds were lovesick with them.   **II.ii.192-194.**

6 Tie up the libertine in a field of feasts,
   Keep his brain fuming.   **II.i.23-24.**

7 He will to his Egyptian dish again. . .   **II.vi.123.**

B   Images of games and pastimes

1 He fishes, drinks and wastes
   The lamps of night in revel.   **I.4.4-5.**

2 What sport tonight?   **I.i.47.**

3 Antony,
   Leave thy lascivious wassails.   **I.iv.55-56.**

4 The very dice obey him
   And in our sports my better cunning faints
   Under his chance . . . .   **II.iii.32-5.**

5 Let it alone, let's to billiards.   **II.v.3.**

6 Give me mine angle, we'll to the river there,
   My music playing far off.   **II.v.10-11.**

7 She, Eros, has pack'd cards with Caesar, and false played my glory
   Unto an enemy's triumph.   **IV.14.19-20.**

8 Here's sport indeed . . .   **IV.xv.32.**

9 And when thou hast done this chare, I'll give thee leave
   To play till doomsday.   **V.ii.320-1.**

10 Your crown's awry,
    I'll mend it and then play.   **V.ii.317-8.**

Activity

Look up the contexts and think about how the force of the imagery increases as they are repeated. Notice, for instance, how the sport idea takes on great poignancy when Cleopatra and her women speak of it in the context of their impending deaths; this would not be so powerful without the earlier establishment of the pattern.

Follow-up

Look for other connected images; this is by no means an exhaustive list. Linked with the first group are a number of images of eating and drinking; these are worth exploring. Antony's faults and qualities are described on a cosmic scale; images of stars and galaxies underline this. His own language, too, draws its comparisons from the same vastness of space and time. Look for examples of these as well.

Collecting these lists of images is not valuable in itself; you need to think about their effect on our perceptions of the characters and ideas.

   Shakespeare: an active approach

27 • Auditions

FOCUS ON: CHARACTER REVISION

SMALL GROUPS

KNOWLEDGE OF PLAY REQUIRED

Procedure

Divide the class into groups of two or three and allocate to each group one character from the play, or two minor ones.

The task is to imagine they are auditioning possible actors for a production. They must choose suitable audition pieces, illustrating different aspects of the character and must decide what voice, tone and appearance they will demand from the performer.

Each group then pairs with another group and sets up 'auditions'. The directing group instructs the 'actors' from the other group about the characterisation they envisage for the part. The 'actors' then try to interpret the chosen speeches or dialogue accordingly.

All these 'auditions' can go on at the same time, each person paired with someone from the opposite group. The most successful can be demonstrated to the rest.

Example

Suggested passages for Caesar are in the Students' Notes. Enobarbus: dialogue with Antony in I.ii. about the death of Fulvia; exchange with Menas at the end of Act II.vii.; his dying speech, IV.ix.11–23.

Follow-up

A piece of writing to follow this could be the director's advice to the actor, using lines from the play as evidence of the points made about character and delivery.

28 • Sequencing: Dialogue

FOCUS ON: PLOT

SMALL GROUP ACTIVITY

KNOWLEDGE OF PLAY NOT REQUIRED

Procedure

This can be done as an introduction to the play, or to reinforce a first reading.

Divide the class into small groups and give them the sheets, explaining that the dialogue boxes are jumbled and have to be sorted into the right order. If you do not want to re-use the sheets, students could cut out the speeches and shuffle them around. If you like, you can prepare several other similar sheets (see suggestions below) so they do not all do the same passage.

Suggest to them before they begin the kinds of clues to look for, i.e. exits and entrances; questions and answers; events and comments on them. This is a surprisingly difficult exercise, even for students who have already read the play, but it does force close attention to the text and far more than a superficial reading of the scraps will have to be undertaken.

When each group is satisfied with its version, they can compare notes about how they reached their conclusions.

Other examples

From ANTONY AND CLEOPATRA: Act.I.iv. Act III.xi.

As long as you bear in mind the difficulty of the activity, any pieces of dialogue from any play can be used. A few photocopies, with judicious use of scissors, is all that is required, but scenes with short speeches and quite a lot of comings and goings seem to work best. Choose an important bit of dialogue so that the extra familiarity with the text will be useful for later discussion. Keep a record of the correct order! The order for the quotations on the students' sheets is **C.B.E.D.A.**

Follow-up

Written work on the piece of text could well follow, especially if the scene is some kind of turning point, on theatrical effectiveness.

27 • *Auditions*

FOCUS ON: CHARACTER/REVISION.

Example

Caesar You may see, Lepidus, and henceforth know,
  It is not Caesar's natural vice to hate
  Our great competitor. From Alexandria
  This is the news: he fishes, drinks, and wastes
  The lamps of night in revel; is not more manlike
  Than Cleopatra; nor the queen of Ptolemy
  More womanly than he: hardly gave audience, or
  Vouchsaf'd to think he had partners. You shall find there
  A man who is the abstract of all faults
  That all men follow.

Caesar Welcome to Rome.
Anthony   Thank you.
Caesar   Sit.
Antony   Sit, sir.
Caesar   Nay, then
Antony I learn, you take things ill which are not so:
  Or being, concern you not.
Caesar   I must be laugh'd at,
  If or for nothing, or a little, I
  Should say myself offended, and with you
  Chiefly i' the world: more laugh'd at, that I should
  Once name you derogately, when to sound
  Your name it not concern'd me.
Antony   My being in Egypt,
  Caesar, what was't to you?
Caesar No more than my residing here at Rome
  Might be to you in Egypt: yet if you there
  Did practise on my state, your being in Egypt
  Might be my question.
Antony   How intend you, practis'd?
Caesar You may be pleas'd to catch at mine intent
  By what did here befall me. Your wife and brother
  Made wars upon me, and their contestation
  Was theme for you, you were the word of war.

Enter OCTAVIA *with her Train.*
Octavia Hail, Caesar, and my lords! Hail, most dear Caesar!
Caesar That ever I should call thee castaway!
Octavia You have not call'd me so, nor have you cause.
Caesar Why have you stol'n upon us thus? You come not
    Like Caesar's sister: the wife of Antony
    Should have an army for an usher, and
    The neighs of horse to tell of her approach,
    Long ere she did appear. The trees by the way
    Should have borne men, and expectation fainted,
    Longing for what it had not. Nay, the dust
    Should have ascended to the roof of heaven,
    Rais'd by your populous troops: but you are come
    A market-maid to Rome, and have prevented
    The ostentation of our love; which, left unshown,
    Is often left unlov'd: we should have met you
    By sea, and land, supplying every stage
    With an augmented greeting.

Activity

Do you feel the speeches/dialogue above are key passages in understanding Octavius Caesar? Which aspects of his character are illustrated here? What is left out? Your group will be allocated a character from the play to look at closely. Imagine you are directing a production and auditioning actors for that part.

Decide between you which passages will best reveal an actor's potential for the role. Keep these passages short and work out how you want them delivered. You have to establish a characterisation for the part which you will convey to 'actors' auditioning for it.

You will then get a chance to try out a member of another group in your pieces (and to audition for one of theirs yourself).

Remember the 'directors' are not judging performances but how well 'actors' respond to their suggestions.

Follow-up

Write your Director's Notes for the character, with comments (constructive) on the potential of your 'actor'.

Keep a note of the passages you chose, as a resource for a future essay or for revision on that character.

  Shakespeare: an active approach **65**

29ᴀ • *Sequencing: Dialogue*

FOCUS ON: PLOT

Example

A

Antony No more light answers. Let our officers
Have notice what we purpose. I shall break
The cause of our expedience to the queen,
And get her leave to part. For not alone
The death of Fulvia, with more urgent touches,
Do strongly speak to us; but the letters too
Of many our contriving friends in Rome
Petition us at home. Sextus Pompeius
Hath given the dare to Caesar, and commands
The empire of the sea. Our slippery people,
Whose love is never link'd to the deserver
Till his deserts are past, begin to throw
Pompey the Great, and all his dignities
Upon his son, who high in name and power,
Higher than both in blood and life, stands up
For the main soldier: whose quality, going on,
The sides o' the world may danger. Much is
        breeding,
Which like the courser's hair, hath yet but life,
And not a serpent's poison. Say our pleasure,
To such whose places under us require,
Our quick remove from hence.
Enobarbus I shall do't.

B

Antony   Forbear me.
                [Exeunt Messengers.
There's a great spirit gone! Thus did I desire it:
What our contempts doth often hurl from us,
We wish it ours again. The present pleasure,
By revolution lowering, does become
The opposite of itself: she's good, being gone,
The hand could pluck her back that shov'd her on.
I must from this enchanting queen break off,
Ten thousand harms, more than the ills I know,
My idleness doth hatch. Ho now, Enobarbus!

Re-enter Enobarbus.

Enobarbus What's your pleasure, sir?
Antony I must with haste from hence.

C

Enter another Messenger.

Antony From Sicyon how the news? Speak there!
First Messenger The man from Sicyon,—is there
        such an one?
Sec. Messenger He stays upon your will.
Antony   Let him appear.
These strong Egyptian fetters I must break,
Or lose myself in dotage.

Enter another Messenger, with a letter.
                What are you?
Third Messenger Fulvia thy wife is dead.
Antony   Where died she?
Third Messenger In Sicyon:
Her length of sickness, with what else more
        serious
Importeth thee to know, this bears.
                [Gives a letter

29ᴮ • *Sequencing: Dialogue*

D

Antony Fulvia is dead.
Enobarbus Sir?
Antony Fulvia is dead.
Enobarbus Fulvia?
Antony Dead.
Enobarbus Why, sir, give the gods a thankful sacrifice. When it pleaseth their deities to take the wife of a man from him, it shows to man the tailors of the earth; comforting therein, that when old robes are worn out, there are members to make new. If there were no more women but Fulvia, then had you indeed a cut, and the case to be lamented: this grief is crown'd with consolation, your old smock brings forth a new petticoat, and indeed the tears live in an onion, that should water this sorrow.
Antony The business she hath broached in the state
Cannot endure my absence.
Enobarbus And the business you have broach'd here cannot be without you, especially that of Cleopatra's, which wholly depends on your abode.

E

Enobarbus Why, then we kill all our woman. We see how mortal an unkindness is to them; if they suffer our departure, death's the word.
Antony I must be gone.
Enobarbus Under a compelling occasion let women die: it were pity to cast them away for nothing, though between them and a great cause, they should be esteemed nothing. Cleopatra catching but the least noise of this, dies instantly. I have seen her die twenty times upon far poorer moment: I do think there is mettle in death, which commits some loving act upon her, she hath such a celerity in dying.
Antony She is cunning past man's thought.
Enobarbus Alack, sir, no, her passions are made of nothing but the finest part of pure love. We cannot call her winds and waters sighs and tears; they are greater storms and tempests than almanacs can report. This cannot be cunning in her; if it be, she makes a shower of rain as well as Jove.
Antony Would I had never seen her!
Enobarbus O, sir, you had then left unseen a wonderful piece of work, which not to have been blest withal, would have discredited your travel.

Activity

These sections have been deliberately jumbled into the wrong order; try to sort the scene into its proper sequence.

Now read it in your order to the others and explain what clues you used to help you sort it out. Finally, check the dialogue in your copy of the play (Act I.ii.).

Follow-up

Comment in writing on the scene you have just been working on. What are its consequences in the later developments of the play? What does it show us of the characters of the speakers? How effective would it be in performance?

 Shakespeare: an active approach **67**

29 • *Prompt Copy*

FOCUS ON: INTERPRETATION

PAIR WORK

KNOWLEDGE OF PLAY REQUIRED

Procedure

The scene chosen is a crucial one, about which critics of the play have often disagreed.

Does Cleopatra really mean to reserve funds and resources for herself and her children, and Seleucus gives the game away? Or is it a 'put-up-job' to convince Caesar that she intends to live so that he will leave her alone and allow her suicide? If it is the latter it certainly works, because he leaves her with her ladies and her first act is to send Charmian for the man with the figs.

Obviously a lot depends on how the scene is played, and one way to bring this out is to ask students to add their own stage directions, about moves and the delivery of lines, together with instructions for the Stage Manager and his or her crew, on lighting and sound.

They should read the scene through, and look up the context and then work in pairs on deciding how it should be staged.

Examples

Another fruitful choice from this play is the scene in the Monument where the dying Antony is brought to Cleopatra and her women (Act IV.xv). It is confusing on the printed page and students will gain a lot from trying to 'move' it; in this case a set plan could accompany the script, on which to mark the moves.

There are many examples in other plays which become clearer when treated in this way: the last scene of HAMLET, for instance, or the opening of KING LEAR.

It helps if you can produce a photocopy of the relevant piece so students can paste it on a larger sheet and have plenty of space to add their extra dimension of theatricality.

Follow-up

Scripts can be exchanged and scenes played out according to the directions given.

29 • *Prompt Copy*

FOCUS ON: INTERPRETATION

Example

Cleopatra [handing a paper] This is the brief:
    of money, plate, and jewels,
I am possess'd of, 'tis exactly valued,
Not petty things admitted. Where's Seleucus?

Enter Seleucus.

Seleucus Here, madam.
Cleopatra This is my treasurer, let him speak, my lord,
    Upon his peril, that I have reserv'd
    To myself nothing. Speak the truth, Seleucus.
Seleucus Madam,
    I had rather seel my lips, than to my peril
    Speak that which is not.
Cleopatra   What have I kept back?
Seleucus Enough to purchase what you have made
        known.
Caesar Nay, blush not, Cleopatra, I approve
    Your wisdom in the deed.
Cleopatra   See, Caesar! O behold,
    How pomp is follow'd! mine will now be yours,
    And should we shift estates, yours would be mine.
    The ingratitude of this Seleucus does
    Even make me wild. O slave, of no more trust
    Than love that's hir'd? what, goest thou back?
        thou shalt

Go back, I warrant thee: but I'll catch thine eyes
Though they had wings. Slave, soulless villain, dog!
O rarely base!
Caesar   Good queen, let us entreat you.
Cleopatra O Caesar, what a wounding shame is this,
    That thou vouchsafing here to visit me,
    Doing the honour of thy lordliness
    To one so meek, that mine own servant should
    Parcel the sum of my disgraces, by
    Addition of his envy. Say, good Caesar,
    That I some lady trifles have reserv'd,
    Immoment toys, things of such dignity
    As we greet modern friends withal, and say
    Some nobler token I have kept apart
    For Livia and Octavia, to induce
    Their mediation, must I be unfolded
    With one that I have bred? The gods! It smites me
    Beneath the fall I have. *[To Seleucus]* Prithee go
        hence,
    Or I shall show the cinders of my spirits
    Through the ashes of my chance: wert thou a man,
    Thou wouldst have mercy on me.
Caesar   Forbear, Seleucus.
                        [Exit Seleucus.

                        from Act V.ii.

Prompt Copy

Cleopatra [handing a paper] This is the brief:
    of money, plate, and jewels,
I am possess'd of, 'tis exactly valued,
Not petty things admitted. Where's Seleucus?

Enter Seleucus.

Seleucus Here, madam.
Cleopatra This is my treasurer, let him speak, my lord,
    Upon his peril, that I have reserv'd
    To myself nothing. Speak the truth, Seleucus.
Seleucus Madam,
    I had rather seel my lips, than to my peril
    Speak that which is not.
Cleopatra   What have I kept back?
Seleucus Enough to purchase what you have made
        known.
Caesar Nay, blush not, Cleopatra, I approve
    Your wisdom in the deed.
Cleopatra   See, Caesar! O behold,
    How pomp is follow'd! mine will now be yours,
    And should we shift estates, yours would be mine.
    The ingratitude of this Seleucus does
    Even make me wild. O slave, of no more trust
    Than love that's hir'd? what, goest thou back?
        thou shalt

Go back, I warrant thee: but I'll catch thine eyes
Though they had wings. Slave, soulless villain, dog!
O rarely base!
Caesar   Good queen, let us entreat you.
Cleopatra O Caesar, what a wounding shame is this.
    That thou vouchsafing here to visit me,
    Doing the honour of they lordliness
    To one so meed, that mine own servant should
    Parcel the sum of my disgraces, by
    Addition of his envy. Say, good Caesar,
    That I some lady trifles have reserv'd,
    Immoment toys, things of such dignity

Handwritten annotations (right-hand margin):

Spit on Cleopatra
all eyes on her.
– from left
Carries scroll.

Turns half right
moves down left.

gesture – here!

– open arms
sits on couch.
Seleucus moves to
back right –

Activity

Read the extract through and remind yourself of the context, then discuss Cleopatra's behaviour here. What is she thinking when she calls on Seleucus as witness? Has she already arranged with him to 'disclose' her secret? Or has she hidden some of her money as an insurance?

Whatever you think is the most likely interpretation here, the actors will have to find ways of conveying that to the audience, in the way the lines are delivered and perhaps in movement and gesture.

Use this script to make your own 'Prompt Copy' of the extract by adding your own stage directions – both for the actors and for the Stage crew about lighting etc.

Follow-up

Summarise your conclusions about this crucial scene in note form and use these notes as a starting point for writing about 'Cleopatra after Antony's death'.

Shakespeare: an active approach **69**

30 • *Hot Seat*

FOCUS ON: CHARACTER

GROUP WORK

KNOWLEDGE OF PLAY REQUIRED

Procedure

Divide the class into groups of five or six. Give each group the same list of important characters, for them to allocate one to each member.

Arrange the seating in an arc for each group, with one chair set apart by itself in the middle.

Each in turn takes this 'Hot Seat', answering questions in rôle while occupying that chair. The rest are the questioners, out of role until it is their turn to take the 'Hot Seat'.

It could help them to find the right sort of questions to ask if you demonstrate the process for a few moments, either by answering in rôle or by asking a few questions of one of the students. They will soon discover that the questions which work best are those which deal with feelings or motives.

Variation: The **Forum** version of this activity has a front person taking the 'Hot Seat' in front of the whole class, with two or three others standing behind his or her chair, fielding the questions from the class in turn.

Example

To Octavius Caesar:

- What were your feelings when you parted from your sister?
- Why did you agree to encourage her to marry a man whom you clearly despised?
- Did you mean to keep your promises to Cleopatra about treating her honourably, or did you always intend to lead her in triumph in Rome if you could?
- Did the scene with Seleucus convince you she had no intention of committing suicide?
- How did you feel when you found her dead?

Follow-up

This will certainly produce plenty of incidental discussion; students are sure to disagree with some of the answers given and may need to check the accuracy of the Hot Seater's memories of the play.

Written work could follow, taking the form of 'stream-of-consciousness', or a soliloquy which Shakespeare did not write, building on the analysis of feelings and motives involved in this exercise.

30 • Hot Seat

FOCUS ON: CHARACTER

Example

It is not always clear exactly what Octavius Caesar is thinking. Cast your mind over the play and find some moments when we are unsure exactly what he is feeling. For instance, what does he think of Lepidus in Act I.vi.? And in Act II.ii. has he already agreed with Agrippa that the suggestion of a convenient marriage with his sister should be proposed to Antony?

Look at Act III.vi: did he intend this ending to the alliance all along? There are many more such questions in our minds, and not only about Caesar of course. There are plenty of questions we could ask other characters as well.

Activity

In your group, allocate one important character from the list to each person. Each in turn occupies the 'Hot Seat' and, while sitting there, answers, in character, questions from the rest of the group. The questioners are out of rôle during this process.

Take time to prepare some really pointed questions: you will find that motivation and reactions to events and people produce the most rewarding answers and the best discussion. If you don't agree with the answers given, discuss them within your group and, if necessary, check your facts from the text.

Follow-up

This can be a good revision exercise, to remind you of both characters and events. Notes made immediately after such an exercise could be very useful for individual revision, especially if you added references to relevant evidence in the text.

31 • *Student as Designer*

FOCUS ON: THEATRE

SMALL GROUP ACTIVITY

KNOWLEDGE OF PLAY REQUIRED

Procedure

Ask students, in twos or threes, to choose a small section from the play and to imagine they are planning a performance of it. They can assume that plenty of theatrical resources are available!

When they have re-read their section, they should plan and draw a setting for it, together with lists of properties and rough designs for costumes. This is best done in groups because of the discussion generated.

They then have to decide on period and style, and the kind of theatrical space they want for their 'performance', and they will need access to reference books and/or photographs of previous productions. (Old R.S.C. programmes are an excellent resource.)

This activity makes students think in theatrical terms and is therefore a useful addition to a predominantly textual study.

Examples

Act IV.i. The Masque gives plenty of scope for exotic design and planning of moves for Prospero and the goddesses.

Act III.iii. is also a good choice, with Prospero 'invisible', Ariel in the form of a harpy confronting the guilty, and Shapes dancing 'with mocks and mows'.

The whole of THE TEMPEST offers particular opportunities to the designer because it is not obviously set in any period and the element of fantasy cries out to be exploited. However, this approach can be used for any of the plays.

Follow-up

Artistic talent is clearly not what you are after but the finished designs will certainly make an excellent and discussion-provoking display. (See also **Prompt Copy** page 68–69.)

31 • *Student as Designer*

FOCUS ON: THEATRE

Example

This illustration shows one interpretation of the play, which as you can see, offers wide scope to the designer. It can be successfully set in any period, and lots of the characters lend themselves to symbolic rather than realistic costume design, e.g. Caliban, Ariel, Prospero.

Activity

Choose one scene or part of a scene to work on. Imagine you are designing a production of the play. In your groups, discuss these questions and decide how your production will be staged.

1 What **kind of theatre** is it to be performed in? Proscenium arch, theatre-in-the-round, a thrust stage, a promenade performance? (If you don't understand any of these terms, look them up in a reference book about the theatre such as the *Penguin Dictionary of the Theatre* or *The Oxford Companion to the Theatre*.)

2 What **period setting**, if any, will bring out the essentials most clearly? Elizabethan, modern dress, or complete fantasy?

3 What **stage set** will allow all the actions and movements necessary to your scene? Do some characters need to be revealed later in the scene? (E.g. Ferdinand and Miranda are discovered playing chess in the last scene.)

4 Can you bring out issues and themes more clearly through **symbolism?** Perhaps, for instance, you feel the audience should be constantly aware of the presence of the sea? How could the design bring this out?

Follow-up

Share your ideas with the rest of the class, perhaps by a wall display. Don't worry if you are not artistic or talented; it is the ideas that are interesting, not the drawings themselves.

Some A-Level questions ask about 'dramatic effect' and, in order to answer these, you have to 'think yourself' into the theatre. This exercise will help.

Royal Shakespeare Company's production of THE TEMPEST, Stratford-upon-Avon, 1982.

32 • Missing Words

FOCUS ON: LANGUAGE

PAIR WORK

KNOWLEDGE OF PLAY NOT REQUIRED

Procedure

Students should work in twos or threes, since the discussion generated is more valuable than the answers they finally come up with; process and not product is important.

Unlike a strictly 'cloze' exercise, this activity demands selection of words for omission, not a regular counted choice of every sixth word.

Try to pick words which are essential to the passage in terms of meaning or imagery, and include a variety of different parts of speech.

Example

Caliban:
All the *infections* that the sun sucks up
From bogs, *fens,* flats, on Prosper fall, and make him
By inch-meal a *disease!* His spirits hear me,
And yet I needs *must* curse. But they'll nor *pinch,*
Fright me with urchin-shows, pitch me i'th' *mire*
Nor lead *me,* like a *firebrand,* in the dark
Out of my *way,* unless he bid'em: but
For every trifle are they set *upon* me;
Sometime like apes, that mow and *chatter* at me,
And after bite me; then like hedgehogs, which
Lie *tumbling* in my barefoot way, and mount
Their *pricks* at my footfall; sometime am I
All wound with *adders,* who with cloven tongues
Do *hiss* me into madness.

Act II.ii 1–14

Follow-up

After they have had time to fill most of the gaps, discuss with them how they reached their choices and what clues they used. They can then compare their versions with Shakespeare's.

This is a good time to introduce some comments on metre and blank verse, as they will have been especially aware of this when making their selections.

The passage could also lead into a closer look at the character of Caliban, and at the 'earthiness' of his language – how it often draws on the animal world, as with the apes, hedgehogs and adders here.

A similar exercise on Ariel's speech, 'I boarded the king's ship. . .' lines 196–206., would provide a useful contrast of vocabulary and style. A photocopier and a little correction fluid make it an easy exercise to prepare.

32 • Missing Words

FOCUS ON: LANGUAGE

Example

Caliban:

All the ___________ that the sun sucks up

From bogs, ___________ flats, on Prosper fall, and make him

By inch-meal a ___________! His spirits hear me,

And yet I needs ___________ curse. But they'll nor ___________,

Fright me with urchin-shows, pitch me i' the' ___________,

Nor lead ___________ like a ___________ in the dark

Out of my ___________ unless he bid 'em: but

For every trifle are they set ___________ me;

Sometime like apes that mow and ___________ at me,

And after bite me; then like hedgehogs, which

Lie ___________ in my barefoot way, and mount

Their ___________ at my footfall; sometime am I

All wound with ___________ who with cloven tongues

Do ___________ me into madness.

Activity

On your own, read through the speech to get the general sequence of thought. Now, working with a partner, try to supply words to fill the gaps. Each gap is one word long and the size of space is no indication of the length of the missing word.

Clues to help you are:
- syntax: you can usually see whether the word is a noun, adjective or verb, or some other part of speech.
- rhythm: you will find that you will know how many syllables the word has by listening to the line.
- vocabulary and images: think of the connections between the ideas in the speech and of the kind of language Caliban uses.

Follow-up

Discuss your choice of words with the rest of the class before you compare your version with Shakespeare's. Which of the clues were most useful in this speech?

Finally, write a paragraph about what we learn of Caliban from this speech.

33 • *Composite Speech*

FOCUS ON: CHARACTER/REVISION

GROUP ACTIVITY

KNOWLEDGE OF PLAY REQUIRED

Procedure

This activity must come after the main study of the play is complete: it is ideal for revision just before the exam.

Divide the students into groups of three or four and allocate one important character to each. Their task is to compile a thumb-nail sketch of the character, using only words drawn from the play, and to present it to the rest imaginatively.

Instructions and ideas are on the Students' Notes, together with a collection of lines about Ariel to illustrate the technique.

Example

Taking Ariel as an illustration, the following are the features which might be included:

1 Ariel's past – imprisonment by Sycorax etc.
2 Bound to Prospero – desire for liberty.
3 What he does at Prospero's command – Alonso and party; Ferdinand; Caliban, Stephano and Trinculo.
4 His songs.
5 Irony that it is he, who is not human, who teaches Prospero to be fully human and to forgive.
6 Prospero's affection for him, and his final freedom.

Follow-up

This is a good preparation for examination questions since it involves students in looking for apt quotations and in selecting the most significant features of the chosen character and his or her relationship with others.

Presentation of the composite speech helps to supply the theatrical dimension to the play, too, and discussion of each performance ensures that everyone is involved in the character analysis of each one.

33 • *Composite Speech*

FOCUS ON: CHARACTER REVISION

Procedure

Here are a number of quotations spoken by, or about, or to, Ariel. See if you can decide why they were chosen and what aspects of the figure of Ariel in the play is illustrated by each.

1 This damned witch Sycorax. . .
   . . . she did confine thee
   By help of her more potent ministers
   And in her most unmitigable rage
   Into a cloven pine.

2 Thou best know'st
   What torment I did find thee in.

3 If thou more murmur'st, I will rend an oak,
   And peg thee in his knotty entrails, till
   Thou hast howled away twelve winters.

4 Full fathom five thy father lies,
   Of his bones are coral made.

5 This music crept by me upon the waters,
   Allaying both their fury and my passion
   With its sweet air.

6 You are three men of sin, whom Destiny
   . . . the never-surfeited sea
   Hath caus'd to belch up you.

7 At last I left them
   I' the filthy-mantled pool beyond your cell,
   There dancing up to their chins.

8 Your charm so strongly works 'em
   That, if you now beheld them, your affections
   Would become tender.

9 Why, that's my dainty Ariel! I shall miss thee.

10 That is thy charge: then to the elements
   Be free, and fare thou well!

Activity

Search through the play for a series of quotations related to your group's character. Some may be spoken by that person, some about him or her, or to him or her, and some may even represent themes and aspects of the play in which he or she is closely involved.

Use the collection of quotations above, about Ariel, as a model, and ensure that each line has some different point to make.

Now devise a way of presenting these lines to form a composite picture of the character. Lines could be delivered in rôle, or in unison, figures could circle the central one as they speak or be placed in different parts of the room.

Try to think dramatically and give the collection of lines some sort of unity; use the space available to best advantage; don't sit round a table and read the lines.

Follow-up

Using the lines you have collected about your character, write an essay on his/her dramatic importance to the play.

34 • *Alternative Viewpoint*

FOCUS ON: CALIBAN

INDIVIDUAL WORK

KNOWLEDGE OF PLAY REQUIRED

Procedure

Close examination of what a particular character knows and sees will improve familiarity with a play. Students will need to discuss the character, and the events which we are told happened before the play opens, and may need some help in finding the relevant scenes and speeches. They could usefully do this in pairs or groups so they can discuss what Caliban feels and thinks and the evidence the play provides, but the writing should be individual. They could write it as a first-person narrative, or as memories related after the end of the play, or in an interior monologue/stream-of-consciousness style.

Other examples

These students' notes refer to THE TEMPEST and Caliban but the technique can be applied to any play.

HAMLET: A recent London production had Ophelia present in several scenes where she is not mentioned in the stage directions, as a silent witness, and this idea could lead to an interesting piece of writing.

Or: Horatio's account, according to Hamlet's dying instructions.

KING LEAR: Perhaps Kent's view? Or the Fool's?

ANTONY AND CLEOPATRA: Enobarbus's view, just before his death, could offer imaginative possibilities.

CORIOLANUS: Events as seen by Virgilia could be interesting even though we would have very little to go on.

Follow-up

A-Level syllabuses frequently offer Coursework options now, and this could prove a way into the creative and imaginative responses often permitted.

34 • *Alternative Viewpoint*

FOCUS ON: CALIBAN

Example

Caliban As wicked dew as e'er my mother brush'd
   With raven's feather from unwholesome fen
   Drop on you both! a south-west blow on ye
   And blister you all o'er!
Prospero For this, be sure, to-night thou shalt have
     cramps,
   Side-stitches that shall pen thy breath up; urchins
   Shall, for that vast of night that they may work,
   All exercise on thee; thou shalt be pinch'd
   As thick as honeycomb, each pinch more stinging
   Than bees that made 'em.
Caliban   I must eat my dinner.
   This island's mine, by Sycorax my mother,
   Which thou tak'st from me. When thou cam'st first,
   Thou strok'st me, and made much of me; wouldst
     give me
   Water with berries in't; and teach me how
   To name the bigger light, and how the less,
   That burn by day and night: and then I lov'd thee,
   And show'd thee all the qualities o' th' isle,
   The fresh springs, brine-pits, barren place and fertile:
   Curs'd be I that did so! All the charms
   Of Sycorax, toads, beetles, bats, light on you!
   For I am all the subjects that you have,
   Which first was mine own King: and here you sty me
   In this hard rock, whiles you do keep from me
   The rest o' th' island.

Activity

Perhaps you feel there is some justice in Caliban's claim to ownership of the island? Certainly, from his point of view, Prospero is unjust (though we learn later of the reasons for this treatment).

Try looking at the play wholly through Caliban's eyes:

First check which scenes he appears in and read these through, thinking at the same time what else he might be aware of, on and around the island (the storm? Ferdinand?).

When you have made some notes for yourself on these scenes, write Caliban's account of the events of the play. Try to capture his tone and type of language (though there is no need to write in blank verse); remember both his curses and his account of the music of the island. (III.ii.133-141.)

Follow-up

What do you think might happen to Caliban at the end of the play? Does he remain behind, or go to Milan? Write his thoughts at the end, or a continuation of his story.

Bob Peck as Caliban in the Royal Shakespeare Company's production of THE TEMPEST, 1982.

35 • Group Soliloquy

FOCUS ON: LANGUAGE

WHOLE CLASS ACTIVITY

KNOWLEDGE OF PLAY NOT REQUIRED

Procedure

The passage given is divided into scraps which have some kind of unity (discrete phrases, syntactical units etc). Allocate one piece to each student or, if necessary, re-divide the passage to fit numbers available – or attempt only part of the passage.

Each student should spend a few minutes saying her or his phrase over in many different ways, according to your instructions; for example, whispering, shouting, greeting other students with it, etc. It also helps if they move around while they're doing this, as this helps them to memorise it. By the end of this process each student should know her or his own bit by heart.

Reassemble the students in a circle in the correct sequence and run through the whole speech so they can learn their cues.

The point of the activity is to create awareness of the theatricality of the script, not to enact the scene from which it comes, so they should be encouraged not to try to deliver the line in character but to allow it to have its own life.

Now the speech should be 'performed' – with movement if possible – to create theatrical effect. They could start at the edges of the room and move in one by one as they deliver the line and finish kneeling in a circle, or they could move round addressing the lines to others in the group.

A pool of light in the centre is a great help to the effect, but a classroom with a little space to move in can work almost as well. Music, too, can add a dramatic dimension and a tape of an Elizabethan pavane or some mysterious synthesiser music can transform the result.

Ask the students to suggest ways to improve the 'performance' and to make the speech more effective.

Examples

Caliban Be not afeard; the isle is full of noises. . .
           . . . I cried to dream again.'   III.ii.133–41

Prospero Our revels now have ended. . .
            . . . is rounded with a sleep.   IV.i.147–58

Any play will offer equally good passages.

Follow-up

Discussion of the language and particularly the imagery will follow naturally. Writing about the speech and what the images contribute is another possible outcome.

35 • *Group Soliloquy*

FOCUS ON:LANGUAGE

Example

Prospero:
Ye elves of hills, brooks, standing lakes, and groves
And ye that on the sands with printless foot
Do chase the ebbing Neptune
                    and do fly him
When he comes back
             you demi-puppets that
By moonshine do the green sour ringlets make,
Whereof the ewe not bites
              and you whose pastime
Is to make midnight mushrooms
                  that rejoice
To hear the solemn curfew
             by whose aid –
Weak masters though ye be – I have bedimm'd
The noontide sun
          call'd forth the mutinous winds
And 'twixt the green sea and the azur'd vault
Set roaring war
        to the dread rattling thunder
Have I given fire
        and rifted Jove's stout oak
With his own bolt
        the strong-bas'd promontory
Have I made shake
        and by the spurs pluck'd up
The pine and cedar
        graves at my command
Have wak'd their sleepers
         op'd, and let'em forth
By my so potent Art
        But this rough magic
I here abjure
      and, when I have requir'd
Some heavenly music
      – which even now I do—
To work mine end upon their senses, that
This airy charm is for
        I'll break my staff,
Bury it certain fadoms in the earth
And deeper than did ever plummet sound
I'll drown my book

*Michael Hordern as Prospero in the Royal Shakespeare
Company's production of THE TEMPEST, 1978.*

Activity

Say your piece of this speech in a lot of different ways to
anchor it in your mind. When you have made the phrase
your own in this way, you will be putting it together with
everyone else's to recreate the speech and 'perform' it
dramatically.

Don't try to act as Prospero or to deliver the line in any
way in character; let the speech take on a life of its own
and make it a theatrical experience in its own right. You
will find this will offer a new insight into the power of the
language, its rhythms and its imagery.

Follow-up

Using the understanding this has given you, write up your
comments on the language of the speech, showing how
the images contribute to its meaning snd how it relates to
the rest of the play.

36 • Ten Years On

FOCUS ON: CHARACTER

PAIR OR INDIVIDUAL DISCUSSION WORK

KNOWLEDGE OF PLAY REQUIRED

Procedure

Projecting a character into the future can provoke discussion and should ensure that students turn to the play for evidence. In the case of Prospero, it seems a fair question to ask what success he will have as Duke of Milan after the end of the play. What has he learnt from his earlier mistakes? What about Antonio and Sebastian? Are there any signs that they have reformed?

Ask students to consider these and the other points mentioned in their notes, and to collect specific evidence from the text to support their views before the discussion begins.

It may be necessary for you to play Devil's Advocate and argue that Prospero will make the same mistakes as before and that, without his magic powers, he will find it difficult to rule successfully.

Other examples

Other plays which lend themselves to the 'ten years on' approach are:

KING LEAR: Albany resigns his power to Kent and Edgar. What sort of rulers will they make and what is there in the play to indicate the qualities/faults each may show?

CORIOLANUS: What will happen in Rome after Coriolanus's death? What will be the thoughts and feelings of the patricians, and especially his family, and of the common people and the tribunes? How will he be remembered?

Follow-up

Discussion can lead on to written work: in THE TEMPEST, Sebastian and Antonio's attitude remains puzzling in the context of reconciliation at the end and is certainly worth a written exploration. The extent of Prospero's dependence on magic and his human compassion (taught him ultimately by a non-human creature) could be a good theme for an essay. Both these would benefit from the above introduction.

Note: A warning is given at the end of the students' notes about not using their projections of the future in A-Level answers. If you think any of your students might fall into this trap, do repeat the warning clearly and make sure it is understood.

36 • Ten Years On

FOCUS ON: CHARACTER

Example

Consider the following lines:

Prospero But this rough magic
I here abjure.   V.i.50-51.

Prospero But you, my brace of lords, were I so minded,
I here could pluck his highness' frown upon you,
And justify you traitors; at this time
I will tell no tales.

Sebastian The devil speaks in him.   V.i.126-9.

Gonzalo And Ferdinand, her brother, found a wife
Where he himself was lost, Prospero his
dukedom
In a poor isle, and all of us ourselves
Where no man was his own.   V.i.210-213.

Prospero . . . And thence retire me to my Milan, where
Every third thought shall be my grave.
V.I.310-311.

Activity

In this last scene of THE TEMPEST there are several reconciliations. Alonso in particular repents his past enmity to Prospero and is linked to him in friendship by the marriage of his son to Prospero's daughter.

Imagine all these characters after ten more years, and consider what might be happening to them then. For instance, what sort of Duke of Milan will Prospero make? (Remember how his brother was first able to seize power.) How will he cope without the aid of his magic?

How will Antonio and Sebastian react to the new regimes in Milan and Naples? Can you find any sign of repentance in this last scene of the play?

What are the prospects for a happy marriage between Ferdinand and Miranda? Is Miranda a trifle naive in her reactions in the final scene? ('O brave new world,/That has such people in it!'.)

Before any general discussion, find evidence from the actual play to support your ideas.

Follow-up

A study of Prospero's character might well start with a consideration of these points; they could also contribute to the favourite A-Level question about the theme of forgiveness and reconciliation in the play. **Remember that your forecast of what is going to happen in the next ten years is not in itself relevant to your A-Level answers, but a means of focusing your attention on aspects of character and initiating discussion.**

Shakespeare: an active approach **83**

37 • *Parallels*

FOCUS ON: INTRODUCTION TO THE PLAY

SMALL GROUP WORK

KNOWLEDGE OF PLAY NOT REQUIRED

Procedure

Choose situations in the play which are capable of some analogy to modern life. It is best to avoid carrying the parallels too far, so focus on a limited section of the story, perhaps one relationship or dilemma. You can tell this mini-story in traditional folk-tale form to remove it from the particulars of time and place ('Once upon a time there lived a king. . . '), or you can transfer it directly to another context (like the film, 'Joe Macbeth').

However you present it to the students, you must emphasise the universal, or even stereotypical elements in it, so they have a wide scope for their analogies. The idea is for them to translate the events and/or characters into a completely new setting.

Ask them to work in twos or threes to devise such a situation and present an improvisation to the rest.

The value of the exercise lies in introducing them to motives and situations which may seem alien in the Shakespeare play but which have some immediacy in another context. There is a danger of over-simplification if parallels are carried too far in the subsequent discussion of the play, but it is a good way in.

Other examples

THE TEMPEST: A wise and learned doctor finds a way of separating the two halves of his personality by drugs into two distinct existences – animal and spirit. . .

MACBETH: The 'Godfather' of a Chicago gang is murdered by his friend and second in command, urged on by an ambitious wife. . .

KING LEAR: An old man wishing to retire from a successful business career hands over control to two daughters and their husbands, who promise him a happy old age with them – but they intend to cut off his income and make him quite dependent on them. . .

HAMLET: Once upon a time there was a great lord, brother to the king of that land, who envied his brother both his power and his beautiful queen. So he began to plan how he could gain both. . .

Follow-up

Discussion should follow when the play is introduced and the situations in the actual play are met; what is different is just as important as what is similar.

37 • *Parallels*

FOCUS ON: INTRODUCTION TO THE PLAY

Example

Once upon a time there was a famous hero who had slain many monsters and enemies and who returned to his people after a great victory, amid much rejoicing. The people of that land wished to honour him by making him a Member of the Council of State, but custom demanded that first he should humble himself by ministering to the beggars of the city in the guise of a poor Friar, for one whole day. This he could not bring himself to do – he was too proud to serve in any way but in battle. So admiration turned to anger and he was finally driven out of his city. . .

Activity

This is a folk tale version of a situation which parallels one in CORIOLANUS; here it is removed from any special time or setting.

Take the basic storyline from this tale and, in your groups, transfer it into a quite different setting of your own. Perhaps the hero could become a modern politician who wishes for power but will not demean himself to win the support of the 'gutter press'? Or he could be a managing director, unwilling to allow his workforce any part in decision-making, who finishes up with a strike on his hands?

Whatever situation you decide on, create an improvised scene to show how your story opens. There is no need to complete the story, just suggest the analogy in one short scene.

Follow-up

Try this parallel to another situation in CORIOLANUS;

Early in the second World War, an anti-Nazi scientist leaves Germany to join the Allies but is unable to take his elderly parents with him. Working on some secret research in England, he discovers that the destination of his new weapon is the city in which his parents live. . .

Develop this as another improvisation in the same way. Later, when you have finished reading the play, you'll be able to compare your situations with Shakespeare's.

Ian Richardson as Coriolanus (centre) in the 1967 production of CORIOLANUS. Royal Shakespeare Company, Stratford-upon-Avon.

38 • Sequencing: Speech

FOCUS ON: TEXT/CHARACTER

PAIR WORK

KNOWLEDGE OF PLAY REQUIRED

Procedure

The students should cut up the sheet of scraps of text, so they can shuffle the pieces.

The activity speaks for itself; it is better done in pairs so there can be discussion about the content and language of the speech, but they could have a few minutes to try it alone first.

When they have agreed on some version, let them check theirs against the original; then move on to discuss the clues they used to sequence it, and the point at which the soliloquy occurs. (It is one of very few soliloquies in this play and is therefore of special interest in the consideration of Coriolanus's character.)

Other examples

Any important speech can be treated in this way. All you need is a photocopy of the piece and a pair of scissors. Stick the fragments on to cards.

Volumnia's pleading with Coriolanus would be a good choice (V.iii.) but might be a bit long and unwieldy unless the segments were quite large; it is a surprisingly difficult exercise.

Another good one would be Coriolanus's speech III.i.90–111, or his attack on the Citizens in I.i.166–87.

The method can of course be applied to any other play.

Follow-up

It is a useful preface to a piece of writing on the speech, of the kind often required by A-Level extract-based questions, e.g. what does the imagery contribute to the passage? What is revealed of the character of the speaker?

38 • *Sequencing: Speech*

FOCUS ON: TEXT/CHARACTER

Example

A 

So with me:
My birthplace hate I, and my love's upon
this enemy town. I'll enter:

B 

Whose hours, whose bed, whose meal and exercise
Are still together, who twin, as 'twere, in love
Unseparable,

C 

Thank you, sir.   Farewell. *[Exit Citizen.*
O world, thy slippery turns! Friends now fast
sworn,
Whose double bosoms seems to wear one heart,

D 

shall within this hour,
On a dissension of a doit, break out
To bitterest enmity:

E 

if he slay me
He does fair justice; if he give me way,
I'll do his country service.

F 

so fellest foes,
Whose passions and whose plots have broke their
sleep
To take the one the other,

G 

by some chance,
Some trick not worth an egg, shall grow dear
friends
And interjoin their issues.

Activity

Can you make sense of this jumbled speech? Use any clues you can find; sentence structure and punctuation; sequence of thought; any connections you can find in the language. It's a good idea to find the opening and the end if you can, and work in to the middle.

The speech is a soliloquy by Coriolanus and occurs when he arrives at Antium in search of Aufidius: this may help you to make sense of it.

When you are satisfied with your version, check it against the original, (IV.iv.11–26.).

Follow-up

You will have examined this soliloquy closely in piecing it together. What do we learn of Coriolanus from it? There are very few soliloquies in this play: why should there be one at this point?

Make notes of your own for future reference.

39 • *Film Adaptation*

FOCUS ON: THEMES AND IMAGES

INDIVIDUAL WORK

KNOWLEDGE OF PLAY REQUIRED

Procedure

Start with a discussion about the opening shots of films and/or TV plays and how the director can use these, sometimes pre-credits, to establish mood and theme, and even to anticipate later events.

The openings of Shakespeare films are particularly useful examples: Olivier's HENRY V, for instance, begins with a sequence which includes a play-bill blowing in the wind and moves into a theatre – thus firmly establishing the 'Let's pretend' of the opening which later merges into 'reality'.

Polanski's MACBETH shows us a windswept and deserted shore, until we close in on the Witches, creating a feeling of the sinister before we hear a word spoken. What must be done largely by words in the play can be suggested by the film-maker in visual images.

After this introduction, encourage them to think of what they want to convey in their opening shots and which details of the play will yield a telling image for the camera. They will then need time to write, perhaps with rough drafts read out from time to time, to help unblock others' ideas.

Other examples

HAMLET: Could begin with night; cold battlements; swirling mist; soldiers on guard; and lead us straight into the opening lines; or the action could be preceded by the funeral of the old king (shots of 'grieving' Claudius and Gertrude?); or there could be a series of images which symbolise later themes and pre-occupations – graves, or a willow growing 'aslant the brook'?

MACBETH: Does not have to follow Polanski: we could see Macbeth and Banquo in battle, or the old king Duncan with his two sons – the old order soon to be displaced –; or it could start with images of darkness and crows making wing to the rooky wood, before cutting to the Witches and the opening lines.

Follow-up

Creative writing on the lines suggested in the Students' Notes can be very successful, or one particular speech from anywhere in the play could be accompanied by detailed camera shots, providing a commentary on the words.

39 • *Film Adaptation*

FOCUS ON: THEMES AND IMAGES

Example

ACT 1

Scene 1

Enter a company of mutinous Citizens, with staves, clubs and other weapons.

First Citizen Before we proceed any further, hear me speak.

All Speak, speak.

First Citizen You are all resolved rather to die than to famish?

All Resolved, resolved.

First Citizen First, you know Caius Martius is chief enemy to the people.

All We know't, we know't.

First Citizen Let us kill him, and we'll have corn at our own price. Is't a verdict?

All No more talking on't; let it be done. Away, away!

Second Citizen One word, good citizens.

First Citizen We are accounted poor citizens, the patricians good. What authority surfeits on would relieve us. If they would yield us but the superfluity while it were wholesome, we might guess they relieved us humanely; but they think we are too dear: the leanness that afflicts us, the object of our misery, is as an inventory to particularise their abundance; our sufferance is a gain to them. Let us revenge this with our pikes, ere we become rakes. For the gods know, I speak this in hunger for bread, not in thirst for revenge.

Second Citizen Would you proceed especially against Caius Martius?

All Against him first. He's a very dog to the commonalty.

Second Citizen Consider you what services he has done for his country?

First Citizen Very well, and could be content to give him good report for't, but that he pays himself with being proud.

Second Citizen Nay, but speak not maliciously.

First Citizen I say unto you, what he hath done famously, he did it to that end: though soft-conscienced men can be content to say it was for his country, he did it to please his mother, and to be partly proud, which he is, even to the altitude of his virtue.

Second Citizen What he cannot help in his nature, you account a vice in him. You must in no way say he is covetous.

First Citizen If I must not, I need not be barren of accusations. He hath faults, with surplus, to tire in repetition.   *Shouts within.*
What shouts are these? The other side o'th city is risen: why stay we prating here? To th'Capitol!

Activity

Imagine you are making a film of CORIOLANUS. Before any dialogue (even, perhaps, before the credits) you wish to create images which will establish mood or make some silent comment on what is to follow. Think about how the play begins; is this how you want to open the film? If so, on which details will you focus?

Perhaps there are other images you would want first? Something to show their motivation, perhaps, or would you want Coriolanus himself to be the first image we see?

You could devise a whole series of shots – in sequence or deliberately disconnected – to symbolise the themes and characters which will follow. For instance, the film could begin with Coriolanus's son destroying the butterfly, as described by Valeria in I.iii. 60–5, to symbolise his father's character. (Notice that a similar image is used to portray the indifference of the Volscians to the fate of the Romans in IV.vi.95–6.)

When you have found suitable shots for the opening, move on to the first lines, above, and specify what might accompany these. There's no need to worry about technical terms as long as you describe briefly the shots you want and whether they should be close-up, or distance.

Follow-up

You will find that with a minimum of editing and revision your list of camera shots can become a poem. Cut out all camera instructions, to leave the images uncluttered, making each picture a separate line and using repetition, perhaps, to make one image recur throughout.

Share your poem with the rest, by reading it out, or making a fair copy for display.

     Shakespeare: an active approach

40 • *Bare Bones: Scene*

FOCUS ON: PLOT

SMALL GROUP WORK

KNOWLEDGE OF PLAY REQUIRED

Procedure

The scene chosen is the one where Coriolanus arrives at the home of his old enemy, Aufidius, and offers his services against his own country. The students' task is to reduce the scene to a three or four minute version, on the lines of Stoppard's *Fifteen minute Hamlet*, in order to concentrate not only on what exactly happens in it but, more importantly, what is lost by this reduction to 'essentials'.

The discussion which follows the performances is the vital part of the activity, and can be a starting point for consideration of the play's language as well as characterisation.

Examples

The principle can be applied to any play; an eventful scene, full of comings and goings works best. Sometimes the result is amusing (the haste and lack of proper transitions parodies the original) but this does not matter if they learn from the experience, and the laughter can lead into useful discussion.

Dumb Show (see pages 56–57) parallels this activity, without words this time.

Follow-up

Choose one section of the scene to use as an extract-based question e.g. lines 59–136. Ask them what imagery contributes to the effectiveness of the passage, and what we learn from it of the characters of Coriolanus and Aufidius.

40 • Bare Bones: Scene

FOCUS ON: PLOT

Activity

Read carefully, in your groups, Act IV.v. Decide what you feel are the most important things which happen in it.

You are going to present this scene in as brief a form as you can, while retaining all important information and characters. You may not improvise the dialogue but must use selected lines from the original, reducing the script to the 'bare bones' but still making it understandable by an audience which may not be familiar with the original.

Remember that the lines will still need to follow logically, though they may well turn out to be somewhat disjointed.

Your version should not take more than three or four minutes to perform.

Follow-up

Discuss what has been lost from the scene in your version. Have you cut out most of the images, for instance, and have the 'lighter' bits disappeared? What would an audience have missed from the original?

Find some examples of lively or vivid language which you have had to cut, and make a note of them for future reference.

Ian Richardson as Coriolanus in the Royal Shakespeare Company's production at Stratford-upon-Avon, 1967.

Shakespeare: an active approach

41 • Obituary

FOCUS ON: CHARACTER

INDIVIDUAL WORK

KNOWLEDGE OF PLAY REQUIRED

Procedure

After a first reading of the play, students can consolidate their views of Coriolanus himself by writing an imaginary obituary for him. They will need to discuss the form first, as some of them may not be familiar with modern obituary columns in the serious papers; they need to realise that achievements and good points are emphasised, but faults not entirely omitted.

It would be a good idea to read them a couple of examples from newspapers, of people recently dead. They also need to decide from what point of view the obituary is to be written.

Other examples

ANTONY AND CLEOPATRA : Antony himself is the obvious choice; Caesar's tribute is generous but by no means covers all the ground. Cleopatra's, too, could prove worthwhile; a balance between her nobility in death and her often petty and devious behaviour earlier would make the obituary interesting reading.

HAMLET : an opportunity here for obituaries of Hamlet from different viewpoints: Horatio's compared with Fortinbras's perhaps?

Follow-up

The newspaper type of exercise tends to be done to death at GCSE-Level and, valuable as it is, it can lack subtlety, but there are variations useful to beginners on an A-Level play – two versions of the same event, for instance, in different types of paper, pro and anti, or possibly editorials commenting on events or behaviour in a thoroughly biased way.

An extra discipline is to rule that the obituary or article must be almost entirely composed of lines from the play, with the minimum of linking words.

41 • Obituary

FOCUS ON: CHARACTER

Example

Aufidius: My rage is gone,
And I am struck with sorrow. Take him up.
Help, three o'th'chiefest soldiers. I'll be one.
Beat thou the drum that it speak mournfully;
Trail your steel pikes. Though in this city he
Hath widow'd and unchilded many a one,
Which to this hour bewail the injury,
Yet he shall have a noble memory.
Assist.

Activity

It is easy to be generous about one's enemies when they are dead, and perhaps this speech of Aufidius' has a touch of this about it. What makes up this 'noble memory'? What do you think were Coriolanus's achievements?

Write down a list of his victories, his brave exploits, and how he dies. Then add his qualities and good points (don't forget the human touch of I.ix.80—4) and find some comments from others in the play which praise him. His faults are clear enough as well; list them also, with suitable quotations.

When you have gathered all this material, use it to write an obituary of Caius Martius Coriolanus, to be published in Rome after his death. Naturally you will emphasise his achievements and qualities, but put in some hints about his faults.

Follow-up

What do you think would be the account of his death in a Volscian newspaper? Write your version of the headlines and a news report, and possibly an editorial commenting on it as well.

Shakespeare: an active approach **93**

42 • Tragic Hero

FOCUS ON: NATURE OF TRAGEDY
INDIVIDUAL WORK/CLASS DISCUSSION
KNOWLEDGE OF PLAY REQUIRED

Procedure

It is always difficult to know how much literary theory to offer to A-Level candidates; it is obviously inappropriate to load them with 'lit. crit.' ideas, but the nature of the tragic experience in the theatre is a real one which they may well have experienced if they have seen performances of the plays, and it therefore demands some consideration.

The extracts from Aristotle are only a starting point, and the discussion will probably have to be largely teacher-led. Concentrate on:

- The mixture of good and evil in the tragic hero;
- The sense of inevitability of the tragic outcome;
- the audience's experience (pity and fear?) throughout the play and especially the sense of reconciliation at the end.

Other examples

KING LEAR: the unusually painful ending needs attention, as does the figure of Cordelia, whose end seems to lack any sense of justice (she is not really a tragic, but a pathetic figure). Also the question of how far Lear brings about his own downfall, by tragic flaw or mistake.

ANTONY AND CLEOPATRA: it is easy to find tragic flaws in both of them but the heroic scale of faults and qualities alike forces us to acknowledge that death can be a victory, and that, in the end, it is 'paltry to be Caesar'. The Aristotle extract is a particularly apt way to initiate discussion of these lines.

Follow-up

There are plenty of essay topics which arise directly out of this discussion, particularly the mixture of faults and qualities which make up the tragic hero.

42 • *Tragic Hero*

FOCUS ON: NATURE OF TRAGEDY

Example

'Tragedy, then is a representation of an action that is worth serious attention, complete in itself, and of some amplitude; in language enriched by a variety of artistic devices appropriate to the several parts of the play; presented in the form of action, not narration; by means of pity and fear bringing about the purgation of such emotions.

. . . It follows in the first place that good men should not be shown passing from prosperity to misery, for this does not inspire fear or pity, it merely disgusts us. Nor should evil men be seen passing from misery to prosperity. This is the most untragic of all plots, for it has none of the requisites of tragedy; it does not appeal to our humanity, or awaken pity or fear in us: Nor again should an utterly worthless man be seen falling from prosperity into misery. Such a course might indeed play upon our humane feelings, but it would not arouse either pity or fear; for our pity is awakened by undeserved misfortune, and our fear by that of someone just like ourselves. . .

There remains a mean between these two extremes. This is the sort of man who is not conspicuous for virtue and justice, and whose fall into misery is not due to vice and depravity, but rather to some error, a man who enjoys prosperity and a high reputation. . .'*

Aristotle: *On The Art Of Poetry*

*The Greek word is 'hamartia', which can mean error or flaw.

Activity

Aristotle wrote these comments about tragedy around 320 B.C., about the tragedies of his own time, so we must be cautious about applying his theories wholesale to Shakespeare's plays, but there are some useful clues here to what can account for the special feeling that tragedy arouses in an audience.

If you have been to see one of Shakespeare's tragedies in the theatre, you will know the feeling we are left with at the end is not complete depression and misery, despite the suffering we have witnessed, but some strange kind of satisfaction at the 'rightness' of events.

You will realise, too, that we feel a mixture of sympathy and criticism for the tragic hero – too much of one or the other destroys the balance – so he must have faults and be, in some measure, the agent of his own downfall, but he must also have redeeming qualities, or we will not care enough what happens to him. We have to think of him, not as an inhuman monster, but a person like ourselves.

Shakespeare's full title for this play is THE TRAGEDY OF CORIOLANUS. Apply some of Aristotle's ideas to the play as a whole, and to Coriolanus himself. What is his tragic fault or flaw? How much sympathy does he arouse in us? Do we feel he is human like ourselves? Does the audience feel that the end is inevitable and 'just'?

Prepare your own notes for a class discussion about the 'tragedy' of this play.

Follow-up

Pride is the essential part of Coriolanus's nature; it is both his vice and his virtue. Write an essay on how it leads to his downfall.

Acknowledgements

Whilst every effort has been made to contact the copyright holders, this has not proved possible in every case.

The author and publishers would like to thank the following for permission to reproduce photographs and illustrations. (The numbers given are page numbers.)

Photographs:
Malcolm Andrews: 41; Angus McBean: 61; Sophie Baker: 39; Donald Cooper: 73, 79, 81; Zoë Dominic: 85, 91; Richard Mildenhall: 29; Nicolas Toyne: 43.

Cover photograph:
Ian McKellen and Judi Dench in the Royal Shakespeare's 1976 production of MACBETH, Joe Cocks Studio.

Illustrations by Peter Kent